£2

THE CONTRACTOR

THE CONTRACTOR

DAVID STOREY

JONATHAN CAPE
THIRTY BEDFORD SQUARE
LONDON

FIRST PUBLISHED 1970
© 1970 BY DAVID STOREY

JONATHAN CAPE LTD
30 BEDFORD SQUARE, LONDON WC1

SBN 224 61899 7

PRINTED IN GREAT BRITAIN
BY EBENEZER BAYLIS AND SON LTD
THE TRINITY PRESS, WORCESTER, AND LONDON
BOUND BY G. AND J. KITCAT LTD, LONDON

FOR KATE

This play was first presented at the Royal Court Theatre, London, on October 20th, 1969, under the direction of Lindsay Anderson. The cast was as follows:

Kay	PHILIP STONE
Marshall	JIM NORTON
Ewbank	BILL OWEN
Fitzpatrick	T. P. MCKENNA
Bennett	NORMAN JONES
Paul	MARTIN SHAW
Claire	JUDY LIEBERT
Glendenning	JOHN ANTROBUS
Old Ewbank	BILLY RUSSELL
Maurice	CHRISTOPHER COLL
Old Mrs Ewbank	ADELE STRONG
Mrs Ewbank	CONSTANCE CHAPMAN

CHARACTERS

KAY, foreman

MARSHALL, workman

EWBANK, the contractor

FITZPATRICK, workman

BENNETT, workman

PAUL, Ewbank's son

CLAIRE, Ewbank's daughter

GLENDENNING, workman

OLD EWBANK

MAURICE, Claire's fiancé

OLD MRS EWBANK

MRS EWBANK

ACT ONE

The stage is set with three tent poles for a marquee, twenty or thirty foot high, down the centre of the stage at right angles to the audience. The poles should be solid and permanently fixed, the ropes supporting them, from the top, running off into the wings. Each pole is equipped with the necessary pulley blocks and ropes, the latter fastened off near the base as the play begins. Two ridge poles, to be used for the muslin, are set between the poles.

Early morning. KAY *enters. He's a big man, hard, in his forties, dressed in working trousers and a jacket, not at all scruffy. He's smoking, just off the lorry, and comes in looking round with a professional eye at the scene, at the poles. He tests one of the ropes, checks another, casual, in no hurry.*

MARSHALL *follows him in a moment later. He's a thin, rather lightweight Irishman, pleasant, easy-going, with no great appetite for work. He's dressed in overalls, well-worn, from age rather than use. He's stretching as he enters, from the ride: arms, legs, back.*

MARSHALL. You put these up yesterday, then, Mr Kay?

(KAY *doesn't answer, going on with his inspection, smoking.*)

(*Calling off*) Aye, Fitzpatrick. If you're bringing in your snap can you bring mine with you?

(MARSHALL *rubs his hands together against a chilly morning, slaps his shoulders, etc.*)

God. This time of the morning. It shouldn't be allowed.

KAY (*indifferent*). Aye.

(EWBANK *has entered. He's a solid, well-built man, broad rather than tall, stocky. He's wearing a suit, which is plain, workman-like and chunky; someone probably who doesn't take easily to wearing clothes, reflecting, perhaps, the feeling of a man who has never really found his proper station in life.*

The jacket of his coat is open as if it's been put on in a rush.)
EWBANK. You've got here, then.
KAY (*looking up*). Morning, Mr Ewbank.
EWBANK. Morning. God Christ. It's bloody afternoon.
KAY. We had some trouble ...
EWBANK (*to* MARSHALL). Look ... look ... look. Mind where you put your bloody feet.
MARSHALL. To God ... (*Moves them in a hurry.*)
EWBANK. That's grass, is that. God Christ, just look at it. (*He presses down a divot.*)
KAY. It must have been from yesterday ...

(FITZPATRICK *enters as* EWBANK *busies himself with looking around and pressing down a further divot.*

FITZPATRICK *is eating a sandwich and in addition to his own bag of food is carrying* MARSHALL'*s, an old army shoulder bag.* FITZPATRICK *is a hard, shrewd Irishman, independent.*)

FITZPATRICK. Is that a ton of lead you have in there, Marshy, or the latest of your mother's buns?

(*He slings the bag to* MARSHALL *who misses it.*)

He couldn't nick a tail off a chocolate mouse.
MARSHALL. Nor a cold off a wet morning!

(*They both laugh.*)

FITZPATRICK (*catching sight of* EWBANK). Oh, good Christ. Good morning. How are you? Good day. Good night ... (*Mumbles on through a ritual of touching forelock, bowing, etc.*)

EWBANK. Mind where you put your feet, Fitzpatrick, or I'll have them bloody well cut off.

FITZPATRICK. Aaaah! (*Steps one way then another. To* MARSHALL) As long as it's my feet only he's after.

(*They both laugh.*)

EWBANK. I came down here ... Are these all you've got? (*Indicating men.*)

KAY (*calling off*). Bennett!

EWBANK. I've never known such a damn place for eating.

> (MARSHALL *as well as* FITZPATRICK *is eating a sandwich*.)

MARSHALL. It's me breakfast ... I haven't eaten a thing all night.

FITZPATRICK. Nor drunk a drop of anything, either.

MARSHALL. Now would I do a thing like that? ... Eating, now, is a different matter.

> (*They both laugh.* BENNETT *has come in carrying a ridge pole on his shoulder.*
>
> BENNETT *is a fairly anonymous person, prefers to be inconspicuous, that is, without being overlooked. He'll do whatever is asked of him, no more and occasionally, if he's sure it'll cause no trouble, a little less. His hair is neatly combed and he wears the trousers of an overall and a clean shirt. He, too, as he enters, carrying the ridge pole, has a sandwich in his mouth and, over his other shoulder, a food bag; in his arms he carries the muslin ropes.*)

BENNETT (*through sandwich*). Quick! Quick! I'm going to drop it ...

EWBANK. Damn and blast it, man, look where you're walking ...

BENNETT. Quick! Quick! It's going on my toes ...

> (*He puts the ridge pole down between the first two vertical poles, groaning and then holding his back as he straightens: evidently the root of all his problems.*)

Oooooooh ... ! I should never ... Oooooooh! (*Holds his back with both hands.*) Rheumatism. Have you ever had anything like it?

EWBANK. Aye. Often.

BENNETT. You have?

EWBANK. When anybody mentions bloody work. I've seen it. Don't worry.

BENNETT. That's right. This place is full of skivers. Just look at that. (*Looks up at the house.*) It's a damn sight warmer in the cab.

EWBANK. I came down, Kay ... Just look at this.
    (EWBANK *has examined where he's laid the ridge pole. Now he presses in another divot.*)

FITZPATRICK. That's a lovely house you have there, Mr Ewbank. (*Gestures off.*)

MARSHALL. Beautiful ... ! Beautiful.

EWBANK. And I'll bloody well keep it that way if I've half a chance.

FITZPATRICK (*to* MARSHALL). He wouldn't be letting us in there, now, that's for sure. To warm up by the fire.

MARSHALL. Toes and fingers ...

FITZPATRICK. Toes and fingers.
    (*They laugh.*)

MARSHALL. Just look, to God. (*Holds up his fingers.*) They're dropping off.

EWBANK. I came down to give you all a warning. Before you start. That house, now, is full of people.

MARSHALL (*looks up*). People ...

EWBANK. Relatives of mine. It overlooks the lawn.

FITZPATRICK. It does. It does. (*To* MARSHALL) How long's he had it?

EWBANK. And I don't want you, Fitzpatrick, up to your usual habits. Piddling all over the place, for one thing, whenever you feel like it. And language. I'd appreciate it very much, Kay, if you saw to it that they watched their tongues.

KAY. Aye. Right.

FITZPATRICK. You do that, Kay.

EWBANK. And for another thing, Kay: this lawn.
    (PAUL *comes in.*)

FITZPATRICK. Don't tell me, now. (*Stoops: examines grass.*) He has.

MARSHALL. Numbered every blade.

FITZPATRICK. Lettered every scratch.

EWBANK. Right. I think you know what's what.

PAUL (*to* KAY, *etc.*). Morning ... Anything I can do ... ?

> (PAUL, *Ewbank's son, is a bit slighter in build than his father, feckless, a little unco-ordinated, perhaps. He's dressed in a shirt and slacks, the former unbuttoned and showing an apparent indifference to the chill of the morning. His initial attitude, deliberately implanted, is that of a loafer. His hands are buried in his trouser pockets and a cigarette hangs, largely unattended, from the corner of his mouth. His manner is a conscious foil to his father's briskness. He has no particular refinement of accent.*)

EWBANK. Aye. You can keep out of the bloody way. Have you had your breakfast?

PAUL. I don't believe ... (*Thinks.*) No. I'm positive. I haven't.

> (*As he talks he drifts over to the poles, examines them, without taking his hands from his pockets, nods to the men, etc., wandering round.*)

EWBANK. You can come in then for that. Kay, I don't think you've met my son?

KAY. No ...

EWBANK. If he gets in the road kick him out of it. It's the only thing he'll understand. Same goes for the rest of the family, too. Get it up. Get it finished. And get away.

KAY (*to* MEN). Right ... Let's have the other ridge ...

MARSHALL. Fitzpatrick ... I reckon it's up to you and me.

KAY (*to* BENNETT). Side poles ...

> (*They go,* MARSHALL *and* FITZPATRICK *still eating.*)

PAUL. I don't mind giving a hand.

EWBANK. Aye, I know what sort of hand that that'll be.

PAUL. I'm very good at this sort of stuff. Though I say it myself.

> (*Takes his hands leisurely from his pockets and, still smoking,*

13

*stoops and lifts the ridge pole a few inches off the ground.
Then he puts it back down.)*

There, then. What did you think to that?

EWBANK. Bloody astonishing. I'd forgotten you'd got hands
on inside them pockets.

PAUL. There's quite a lot of things I've got you haven't seen.
I don't know. Some of them might surprise you.

EWBANK (*to* KAY). Surprises. I live from one minute to the
next. (*He laughs.* KAY *gives no expression.*)

(*There are frantic wolf-whistles off.*

CLAIRE, *Ewbank's daughter, comes in. Slightly younger
than* PAUL, *easy-going yet never anxious to be imposed-
upon. She's wearing jeans and a sweater which show a
regard for practicality rather than fashion. Pleasant. Acts
tough.*)

CLAIRE. They've started, then.

EWBANK. That's right. They have. Just about.

CLAIRE. How long'll they take? (*Looks at poles, ropes.*)

EWBANK. All day and a bit beyond if you can't keep clear.
Now come on. Get in. This's no place here for you ... The
lucky bride, Kay.

KAY. How d'you do? (*Laying out the muslin ropes*)

EWBANK. How many lasses have you got, Kay?

KAY. Four.

EWBANK. Four! To God. One is well enough for me.

(EWBANK *puts his arm affectionately about her shoulder.*)

One of each, and they've skint me afore I'm fifty.

PAUL. I don't know. There's still a bit to go.

EWBANK. Aye. So they say. So they tell me.

CLAIRE (*to* KAY). If there's anything you want just let us
know. In the house, I mean.

KAY. Right ...

PAUL (*stooped, hands in pockets*). And if you want an extra
hand ...

14

KAY. Aye.

CLAIRE. Yours truly ... (*Laughs, indicating* PAUL.)

PAUL (*to* CLAIRE). They don't believe me. I'm bloody good at this.

EWBANK. Don't worry. If Kay wants any help he knows where to look for it ... (*To* KAY) I'll leave you to it. I'll pop back in half an hour.

KAY. Aye. All right.

PAUL (*to* CLAIRE). D'you wanna fag?

CLAIRE. No thanks ...

PAUL. Me last one. (*Coughs heavily, to amuse her.*)

EWBANK (*going, confidential to* KAY). I don't mind so much about the piddling. It's just with the house. I have me mother here, you know. And my old man.

KAY. Aye. I understand.

EWBANK. You've got to be able to look out of your own front window, Kay. You understand?

KAY. I'll keep an eye on them.

EWBANK (*looking round*). A grand day for it. No wind. A bit of sun ...

KAY. Aye ...

EWBANK (*going, arm round* CLAIRE). Well, lass, how're you feeling?

CLAIRE. Champion.

EWBANK (*pleased*). Champion, is it?

CLAIRE. Aye. That's right.

> (*They go.* CLAIRE *laughing,* PAUL *slouching along with deliberate affectation behind, casting a glowering look at* KAY, *coughing, before he finally goes.*
> *During their departure other sounds have started up outside from Marshall and Fitzpatrick.*)

MARSHALL.⎫ Hup, three. Hup, three. Hup three. Hup, hup,

         ⎬ hup ... two, three, four. Hup, hup, hup, hup.

FITZPATRICK.⎭ Hup ... two, three, four. Hup, hup, hup, hup.

15

(*They enter carrying a ridge pole between them on their shoulders. It's quite light, but they make a routine of it, as if on parade, each carrying at the same time a sandwich in their free hand.*)

MARSHALL. Four, five, six ...

FITZPATRICK. Left, left, left ...

MARSHALL (*to* KAY). Is that Ewbank's daughter, then?

KAY. That's right.

FITZPATRICK. Good Christ ...

MARSHALL. Aye, now ...

FITZPATRICK. How could something as beautiful as that come out of something so repulsive?

(MARSHALL *laughs. They've put the pole down between the uprights.*)

KAY (*going*). All right, then. Let's have the canvas off ...

(KAY *goes.*)

FITZPATRICK. Nay, steady on, Kay. I've just done a spot of work. It's freezing. Let's have a little look around. Now, then ... There's the town, from which, earlier in the day, unless I'm mistaken, we ascended. Covered, I'm sad to say ... (*Stoops to peer at it more closely.*) by a cloud of smoke.

MARSHALL. Impenetrable. (*Eating his sandwich*)

FITZPATRICK. Not a spot of anything ... (*Eating too*)

MARSHALL. On a clear day though ...

FITZPATRICK. Oh, the view, Marshy, is magnificent. Quite worth the effort, I'd imagine, of coming all the way up here to work.

(BENNETT *has come in, dropping down a quantity of side poles.*)

BENNETT. Is that Ewbank's son, then?

FITZPATRICK. Is that his daughter?

(*They laugh.* KAY *has returned, bringing in a quantity of side poles which he lays down.*)

Who's she getting married to, then? (*To* KAY.)

KAY. I've no idea. (*Goes off.*)

FITZPATRICK. A university man if ever I saw one. (*Still eating his sandwich*)

BENNETT. Who's that, Fitzie? (*He's shackling the muslin ropes to the muslin ridges.*)

FITZPATRICK. The son.

MARSHALL. The mark of an educated man.

FITZPATRICK. Unlike his bloody old man.

> (*They laugh.*
> KAY *comes back with more side poles.*)
> An intellectual. (*Taps the side of his head knowingly.*) You can tell it at a glance.

MARSHALL. Never done a day's work in his life.

> (*They laugh.*)

BENNETT. A house like that, and you don't need to do any work ...

MARSHALL. Built up from what ... ?

FITZPATRICK. The money he never paid us ...

BENNETT. And a damn sight more besides.

FITZPATRICK (*gestures*).

> The windows bright with our sweat
> The concrete moistened by our sorrows.

MARSHALL. Did you get that out of the paper?

FITZPATRICK. I did.

KAY. Bloody eating. I've never seen such a place for food. Where's Glendenning? (*Checks* BENNETT'*s shackling of the muslin ridges.*)

BENNETT. He's fastening up the gates.

FITZPATRICK (*imitating, suddenly, a wild and vicious man*). 'Will you keep the gate shut, damn you! Haven't I enough trouble in here wid'out you letting more in besides?'

MARSHALL. Is that what he said? (*Looks up at house.*)

FITZPATRICK. That's right, Kay, isn't it?

(KAY *doesn't answer but goes on working.*)

No sooner got the poles up than he comes tearing across the lawn, the dogs yapping at his heels. 'Who the hell left that damn gate open?' I thought he'd fire him on the spot.

MARSHALL. No such damn luck, I'm thinking.

FITZPATRICK. No: no such damn luck. You're right.

(*They laugh. The tone of this, directed as much at KAY as at anyone else, is that of a casual effort to fill in time, to smoke, eat, etc.*)

BENNETT. He's not a man to provocate.

(*They laugh.*)

KAY. He's a man to come back down here in half an hour. Come on. Come on ... Glendenning, where the *hell* are you going with that?

(GLENDENNING *is perhaps in his early twenties, a good-natured, stammering half-wit. He wears overalls, well-worn but scrupulously clean, and considerably too large for him. A big pair of boots stick out from underneath; something, alto-gether, of a caricature of a workman. He has entered, carrying a fourteen-pound sledgehammer over one shoulder, and several marquee stakes over the other, crossing over the stage towards the other side.*)

GLENDENNING. I ... I ... I ... I ... I ... I ...

MARSHALL (*sings to tune of 'Down Mexico Way'*). Ay, yi, yi, yi ... Ay, yi, yi, yi!

GLENDENNING. I ... I ... I ... I'm going to n ... n ... n ... *nnnnn* ... knock in some ... *sssss* ... stakes.

BENNETT. Stakes!

FITZPATRICK. Stakes, bejesus.

KAY (*matter of fact*). You bloody idiot.

GLENDENNING. W ... wwww ... what?

MARSHALL. He said: 'You bloody idiot.'

GLENDENNING. Wa ...

18

BENNETT. The stakes, man. The stakes.

(GLENDENNING *looks at the stakes. He gazes at them for a while.*)

GLENDENNING. W ... wwww ... what?

KAY (*going, casual*). Fitzpatrick. Bennett ... Come on, now. Come on. (*He goes.*)

FITZPATRICK. You don't knock stakes in here.

MARSHALL. You don't at all.

GLENDENNING. What? (*He looks up at the poles.*)

BENNETT. Not in Mr Ewbank's lawn.

MARSHALL. No, no.

FITZPATRICK. He's planted this, he has, with special grass. (*Gestures at house.*) You've to step over it ... like walking on a cloud. Here, now. Here. Look at this ...

(FITZPATRICK *tiptoes to and fro so that* GLENDENNING *might see.*)

KAY (*off*). Fitzpatrick ...

FITZPATRICK. Come on, now. Let's see you do it.

MARSHALL (*indicating house*). If you can't do it, you know, he'll not have you near the house.

FITZPATRICK (*doing it himself*). Come on, now. Like this ...

MARSHALL. Do you know what he'll do?

GLENDENNING (*uncomprehending*). W ... wwww ... what?

MARSHALL. If he looks through his window and sees you walking about with stakes dangling from your arm?

(GLENDENNING *is uncertain, looking from one to the other. Then:*)

GLENDENNING. N ... nnnn ... no.

FITZPATRICK. He'll come out here ...

BENNETT. And take that hammer ...

MARSHALL. And drive one right through your ...

GLENDENNING. Oh!

(MARSHALL *has placed a forefinger to each of* GLENDENNING's *temples, pinning his head between.*)

19

FITZPATRICK. Come on, now. Let's see you do it.

MARSHALL. You have to pass the test!

BENNETT. If he's watching, he might just change his mind.

> (FITZPATRICK, *with something of a gesture, poses on his toes.*
>
> GLENDENNING *looks at them, then up at the house.*)

FITZPATRICK. Up, now ... Higher.

GLENDENNING. I can't ...

MARSHALL. Oh, now. That's not so bad.

FITZPATRICK. He'll be very pleased with that.

> (GLENDENNING *has scarcely raised his heels.*)

MARSHALL. He will. I haven't a doubt.

FITZPATRICK. That's the best piece of toe-walking I've seen in all my life.

BENNETT. For many a year.

MARSHALL. For many a year. You're right.

FITZPATRICK. Do you know, now, what I think he'll do ...

KAY (*off*). Bennett ... !

MARSHALL. He'll come out here ...

> (GLENDENNING *still poses, watching them.*)

BENNETT. 'Glendenning', he'll say ...

FITZPATRICK. 'As a special favour to myself—to myself, mind—I'd be very grateful if you'd come down here each morning ... '

GLENDENNING. M ... mmmm ... morning.

MARSHALL. 'To my house ... '

FITZPATRICK. 'For it just so happens I've been looking for a man the very likes of you ... '

MARSHALL. 'A special person ... '

GLENDENNING. Sp ... sp ... sp ... sssss ... special.

BENNETT. 'For a job, that is, I have in mind ... '

FITZPATRICK. 'And for which it seems to me you have all the necessary qualifications.'

GLENDENNING. Aye!

MARSHALL. Aren't you going to ask him what it is, Glenny?

GLENDENNING. Aye!

FITZPATRICK. Do you see, now, all those little holes ...

GLENDENNING. Aye!

FITZPATRICK. Lying all over the grass ...

GLENDENNING. Aye!

FITZPATRICK. Each one, you know, has a little worm inside.

GLENDENNING. Aye!

FITZPATRICK. And every time it pops its head out ...

GLENDENNING. Aye!

FITZPATRICK. I want you to hit it. As hard as you can. With that. (*Indicates hammer.*)

> (*They laugh.* GLENDENNING, *not at all put out, gazes round at them with a broad smile, pleased.*
> KAY *comes back carrying 1st bag of canvas. He dumps it down.*)

KAY. Bennett. Let's have the canvas off. Fitzpatrick.

FITZPATRICK. Aye, aye, sir.

KAY. And easy with it as it comes. (*To* GLENDENNING) You better put those back, lad.

GLENDENNING. H ... hhh ... How're you going to k ... kkkk ... keep it up?

FITZPATRICK (*going*). That's a very philosophical question ...
> (*He and* MARSHALL *go off, laughing.* MARSHALL, *a moment later, however, comes back.*)

MARSHALL. Ay, now. He didn't mention me at all.
> (*Put out, he potters with the ropes, checking them with no interest at all.*)

KAY (*patiently to* GLENDENNING). Mr Ewbank, now— he's asked us to put no holes into his lawn. (*Presses lawn with his foot to demonstrate its quality.*)

GLENDENNING. Aye!

MARSHALL. We're going to float it up, Glenny. If we all

stand here, now, and puff together ... I think we'll be all right.

KAY (*to* MARSHALL). Come on. You can lift a piece with me ... (*as they go*) You want to leave Glendenning alone. Have you heard that, now?

MARSHALL. Me? Me? I've never even touched him ... (*to* FITZPATRICK *coming in*) Have you heard him, now? They're blaming me. Not a damn minute's rest here for anyone.

> (FITZPATRICK *and* BENNETT *are carrying in the 2nd bag of canvas.*)

FITZPATRICK. We've left the heaviest piece behind.

MARSHALL (*going*). What?

FITZPATRICK. Couldn't shift it, man. Needs a great big feller like yourself.

MARSHALL. Oh, to God, now: every time.

> (MARSHALL, *groaning, follows* KAY *out.* FITZPATRICK *and* BENNETT *dump the canvas on the first ridge pole.* GLENDENNING *watches, nodding, smiling.*)

BENNETT. We'll have some trouble here.

FITZPATRICK. What's that?

BENNETT. Running the guys back to the house.

FITZPATRICK. As a matter of topicality. And (*indicating* GLENDENNING) between ourselves. What are we going to fasten them to?

> (*They're unlacing the bag, getting the canvas out, obviously familiar with the job.* KAY *and* MARSHALL *return with the 3rd bag of canvas, for the rear end of the tent.*)

BENNETT. You remember yesterday?

FITZPATRICK. Do I not?

BENNETT. After we'd put the poles up and you'd gone back to the yard?

FITZPATRICK. I do. Work for me, Benny, at least, had finished.

BENNETT. He had Kay and myself knocking stakes into ...
   Can you guess?

FITZPATRICK (*looks round. Then:*) I can not.

BENNETT. The beds.

FITZPATRICK. The beds.

BENNETT. Each one disguised, very nearly, as a flower.

FITZPATRICK. The cunning bastard.

BENNETT. Do you remember the time ... ? (*Spreading the canvas*)

FITZPATRICK. I do.

BENNETT. When he made us put up that marquee in a gale at
   Arsham?

MARSHALL (*spreading out the 2nd bag of canvas with* GLEN-
   DENNING). The time it blew away?

FITZPATRICK. 'Come back! Come back wid' you! Come
   back!'
      (*They laugh.*)

MARSHALL. He's a very funny feller.

FITZPATRICK. He's amusing, right enough.

KAY. Get it out. Get it out.

FITZPATRICK. What? Right here?
      (*They laugh.* BENNETT *and* FITZPATRICK *have spread
      out the canvas, neatly, either side of the ridge pole.*

      MARSHALL *and* GLENDENNING *are doing the same.*

      KAY *is shackling and spreading the 3rd piece.*

      *Gradually, in spite of their chatter, the pace of work has
      begun to assert itself.*)

MARSHALL (*to* GLENDENNING). No, this way, boy. This
   way.

BENNETT. Have you noticed?

FITZPATRICK. What? What? What?

BENNETT. New. All of it. (*Indicating canvas, which is clean and
   white*)

KAY. He's had the canvas specially made.

MARSHALL. He has. You're right.

FITZPATRICK. Just look now at this stitching. Beautiful.

MARSHALL (*to* GLENDENNING). We'd never get a tent like that, Glenny, if you or I were wed.

BENNETT. And how long have you been married?

MARSHALL. Married? Longer than you can count.

(BENNETT *laughs disbelievingly*.)

FITZPATRICK (*faltering*). W... w ... w ... One ... T ... t ... t ... Two.

(*They laugh.*

They've begun to attach the rings, fastened to the necks of the canvas, round the poles. They're secured with a bolt, like a collar. The collar itself is then shackled to the pulley rope above and the ridge pole underneath. The guys they fasten off to the 'pegs' in the wings.)

BENNETT. Been a bachelor, he has, all his life.

MARSHALL. I have not.

FITZPATRICK. A Protestant agnostic, Marshy. (*Indicating* MARSHALL)

MARSHALL. That I am ...

FITZPATRICK. Of mixed parentage, and of a lineage so obscure it'd defy a mouse to unravel it — has been married three times already.

MARSHALL. That I have.

FITZPATRICK. Once to a lady bus-conductor.

MARSHALL. That's right.

FITZPATRICK. Once to a greengrocer's right-hand assistant.

MARSHALL. That is correct.

FITZPATRICK. And once, would you believe it, to a nun.

MARSHALL. She was not.

FITZPATRICK. I could have sworn you said she worked in a convent.

MARSHALL. I did. But she wasn't a nun.

FITZPATRICK. Good God. I hate to think what it is, now, you've been up to.

MARSHALL. She worked inside. In the kitchens.

FITZPATRICK. In the kitchens. No wonder, to God, he's so fond of food.

MARSHALL. I am! Eatin', now, is one of life's greatest pleasures!

> (*They laugh.* FITZPATRICK *has been fastening off the guys; so has* GLENDENNING. *The others are working at the shackles at the foot of the poles.*
>
> OLD EWBANK *has come on. In his late sixties, wearing a tweed suit: gnarled. An old artisan. He wanders across absent-mindedly, lighting his pipe.*)

OLD EWBANK. Have you seen an old piece of rope lying around? ... About this length.

MARSHALL. What?

OLD EWBANK. Here. About this thick. (*Makes a circle thumb and finger which he adjusts with some with care.*)

MARSHALL. No, no. I don't think I have ...

OLD EWBANK. Water? You couldn't rot it if you tried.

MARSHALL. Oh ...

OLD EWBANK. No damn stamina. Resilience: nothing.

> (*He walks off.*)

FITZPATRICK. And who the hell was that?

MARSHALL. I've no idea. (*Laughs.*)

FITZPATRICK. Well, now. This is the funniest place I've ever seen.

KAY. Right, then ... let's have it up.

FITZPATRICK. Up?

MARSHALL. Up.

FITZPATRICK. Glenny, now—that's you he means.

> (*They laugh.*)

KAY. Right, then. Shoulder height ... fasten off.

(*Between them, having spread out the canvas—two middle pieces and an end—they haul it up to shoulder height, the sections fastened together by the collars.*

They fasten the ropes off, through holes in the base of the tent poles, and begin to lace the sheets of canvas together.

MARSHALL *sings, begins to whistle, then:*)

FITZPATRICK. There was this place, now ... where was it? ... where this feller came in with a little can.

BENNETT. A can?

FITZPATRICK. A can. Full of ... where were we?

MARSHALL. Full of pennies.

FITZPATRICK. Pennies. Asked Ewbank if he could give him one.

(*They laugh.*)

Miles from anywhere ... wanders up ...

MARSHALL. 'Have you got one, then, mister?' ... shakes his can.

FITZPATRICK. Ewbank ...

MARSHALL. Should have seen him.

FITZPATRICK. Green to purple vertigo in fifteen bloody seconds.

(*They laugh.*)

Picks up a hammer ... 'Here, then ... '

MARSHALL. Fifty bloody stakes.

FITZPATRICK. Shoves them in his hand ... 'Here, now. There's a penny ... knock them in, and I'll pop one in your can.'

(*They laugh.*

They're all lacing now, except FITZPATRICK *who has threaded the muslin rope through the loop hanging from the downstage ridge pole.*)

GLENDENNING (*lacing*). If my d ... d ... d ... daughter ...

MARSHALL. Aye, aye, aye. What's that?

GLENDENNING. If my d ... d ... d ... daughter ...

FITZPATRICK. If his daughter. I never knew you had a daughter, Glenny ...

MARSHALL. Nor even a mother.

FITZPATRICK. Nor even a dad.

(*They laugh.*)

BENNETT. Where did you find her, Glenny?

FITZPATRICK. In your wage packet on a Friday night.

(*They laugh.*)

MARSHALL. If you had a daughter, Glenny?

GLENDENNING. I'd like her go ... g ... get m ... m ... *mmmm* ... married ... in one of these.

MARSHALL. You would?

GLENDENNING. Aye!

FITZPATRICK. On top, Glenny, or underneath?

(*They laugh.*)

BENNETT. Wearing it, Glenny? (*Showing him*) Or underneath?

GLENDENNING (*uncertain*). Aye ...

FITZPATRICK. Ah, well. One day, Glenny.

GLENDENNING. Aye. (*He smiles shyly.*) Aye.

(FITZPATRICK *takes his place at the lacing.*)

KAY. Glendenning ... (*Calls* GLENDENNING *over to take his place.*) Get on with it, Bennett. (*Going*)

BENNETT. It's always me. Always me. Did you notice that? It's always me he's after.

(KAY *has gone off.*)

FITZPATRICK (*lacing*). Kay, you know, is a married man.

(*They look off as they work.*)

MARSHALL. He is?

FITZPATRICK. He has four daughters, each one of them a bit bigger than himself.

BENNETT. D'you hear that, Glenny? There might be one of them in there for you.

GLENDENNING. Ah ... I w.w ... w.w ... w.w ... wouldn't want one of Kay's lasses.

MARSHALL. Which one would you like, Glenny?

GLENDENNING. I w ... w ... wouldn't mind the one they have in theer. (*Gestures at house.*)

(*They laugh.* GLENDENNING *is very pleased.*)

BENNETT. She's already spoken for is that, Glenny.

FITZPATRICK. Though I'm thinking if she hasn't set eyes on Glenny here she might very well change her mind.

(*They laugh.*)

GLENDENNING (*carried away*). Th ... th ... th ... there's many a slip twi ... twi ... twi ... twixt c ... c ... c ... cup and l ... l ... l ... l ... lip!

BENNETT. There is, lad. There is.

MARSHALL. Now then, where have I put me rubber hammer? (*Looking anxiously round*) Me hammer, Glenny. And me glass nails.

GLENDENNING. Sh ... sh ... sh ... shall I look in the cab?

MARSHALL. Aye. Aye, you do that. I'll be in a fix without—

BENNETT. Glass hammer in the cab, Glenny. And rubber nails in the back.

(GLENDENNING *goes.*)

FITZPATRICK. Aye, now. That's a sight that'd turn a donkey round.

(KAY *has come in with a huge bag of walling on his shoulder. Tip it down at one side. With him, too, he's brought the four quarter guys.*)

KAY. Come on. Come on. Haven't you finished yet? Where's Glendenning wandering off to?

MARSHALL. He's fallen in love, Kay.

FITZPATRICK. With the lady of the house.

(*They laugh.*)

MARSHALL. She was only a tentman's daughter
But she knew how to pull on a guy.

KAY. Glendenning: come on, here!

(GLENDENNING *has come back on.*)

MARSHALL. Ay, now, Ay, now. I believe he hasn't found it.

BENNETT. Did you get it, Glenny?

FITZPATRICK. Don't tell me I'll have to do without.

(GLENDENNING *laughs, indicating he's seen the joke.*)

MARSHALL. Here I am now, stuck waiting. Can't move another step without.

(GLENDENNING *shakes his head, still laughing, swaying from side to side, his hands hanging, clenched, before him.*)

KAY. Get all the guys fastened off, Glendenning.

(*They go on lacing up the canvas which is done by threading loops from one side through eyelets on the other.*

KAY *positions and fastens on the quarter guys.*)

FITZPATRICK. Ay, now. I'm dying for a smoke.

MARSHALL. Do you think they're watching from the windows? (*Looking at the house*)

FITZPATRICK. Do I not?

MARSHALL. Toes and fingers.

FITZPATRICK. Toes and fingers.

KAY. *Glendenning!*

BENNETT. Bloody cold. Just look. (*Shakes his fingers.*)

(GLENDENNING *is still standing there, swaying, grinning. The men turn round to look.*

BENNETT *has finished his lacing and has gone over to finish* GLENDENNING'*s.*)

KAY. What the *hell*, Glendenning, do you think you're doing?

(GLENDENNING *still grins.*)

MARSHALL. Ay, Glenny, lad, you don't want to get the old feller upset.

GLENDENNING (*pleased*). I w.w.w … w.w.w … w.w.w …

BENNETT. Nay, Glenny …

GLENDENNING. You're nnn ... nnnn ... not going to trick mmmm ... mmmm ... me again!

KAY. I said fasten off the ropes.

GLENDENNING. You're mmmm ... going to mmmm ... blow it up. Mmmmm ... Marshall told me.

KAY. God Christ.

> (KAY *unlaces the walling bag, forestage. He turns away in disgust. The others laugh, more to themselves in order not to provoke* KAY *unduly.*)

Bloody lunatics. It'll be the day in this place when they hire a bloody man.

MARSHALL. Now, Glenny. You've got Mr Kay upset.

> (GLENDENNING *nods, smiling broadly.*)

FITZPATRICK. Nay, nay, Glenny, lad. No joking. Mr Kay wants you to examine all the ropes. The stakes are hidden in the flower beds. Just see if they're fastened on ... One little rope now round each petal.

> (*They laugh.* GLENDENNING *smiles confidently, pleased, still swaying, his hands clenched before him.*)

KAY. You see how it ends up, Fitzpatrick. Rubber nails. Glass hammers.

MARSHALL. Nay, fair's fair. Glass nails it was.

FITZPATRICK. And a rubber shaft.

> (*They laugh.*)

KAY. You go, Marshall. You started it.

MARSHALL. What?

> (*The men laugh as* MARSHALL *sets off to fasten on the guys.*)

There's only one person does any work round here. (*To* GLENDENNING) Can't you see? Stuck in front of you. Geeee ... ! (*Smacks his hand against his own forehead.*)

> (*The men laugh,* FITZPATRICK *doubled up.*)

KAY (*indicating lacing*). Pull it tight. Pull it tight.

FITZPATRICK (*to Marshall*). Pull it tight, Marshy.

MARSHALL. Pull it tight I shall.

(BENNETT *laughs.*

They've begun to put in the side poles now: one at each corner of the tent, and four more at the 'quarters'. i.e. at the point where the laced edges meet. On to these quarter poles they fasten the quarter guys, already clipped to the 'pegs' by KAY.)

FITZPATRICK. Have you seen his wife?

(BENNETT *looks round.* FITZPATRICK *gestures at the house.*)

Ewbank's.

BENNETT. Don't think I have.

(MARSHALL *laughs.*)

FITZPATRICK. If I had a wife like that I wouldn't spend my time, now, making tents.

BENNETT. No?

MARSHALL. Concrete shelters, I should think more likely. (*They laugh.*)

FITZPATRICK. What do you say, Kay?

KAY (*putting in the downstage corner pole* — FITZPATRICK *is putting in the other*). Either way, one wife, after a couple of years, is very much like another.

FITZPATRICK. Is that so, now. Is that a fact?

KAY. It is.

FITZPATRICK. You've seen old Ewbank's wife, then, Marshy?

MARSHALL. What? What? Where's that? (*Looking quickly round*)

(*They laugh.*)

FITZPATRICK. Bloody nig-nog, man.

MARSHALL. Oh. Aye.

FITZPATRICK. You don't think much to her, Marshy?

MARSHALL. Do I not? (*Laughs.*)

FITZPATRICK. Seen better, have you, Marshy?

MARSHALL. Seen better? I should think I have.

BENNETT. And where would that be, Marshy?

MARSHALL. Around, I think. Around.

BENNETT. Around? Around where, then, Marshall?

MARSHALL. One or two places I have in mind.

(*They laugh.*)

BENNETT. The places Marshall hangs around I'd be surprised
if you'd find a woman there at all.

FITZPATRICK. Is that a fact, now, Benny. I'm not so sure of
that.

MARSHALL. Won't find Bennett there, now: that's for sure.

FITZPATRICK. Find Bennett some places I wouldn't care to
mention.

(*They laugh.*)

Seen him one night ... now, where was it? ... taking out
his dog.

MARSHALL. A dog!

FITZPATRICK. Fine little mongrel ... Black and white, now ...

MARSHALL. Wags its tail.

FITZPATRICK. Wags its tail, you're right.

KAY. Right, then ... are you ready? Let's have you underneath.

(*The canvas has been stood up now around the edges and the
men have started scrambling underneath, moving on all fours
to get to the ropes by the poles.*)

FITZPATRICK (*underneath*). Ay, get off! Get off!

(*There are cries and laughs as they horse around.*)

BENNETT (*underneath*). What're you doing ...

MARSHALL (*underneath*). Aaaah!

FITZPATRICK (*underneath*). Get off! Get off!

BENNETT (*underneath*). Give over!

(*A burst of laughter.*)

KAY (*underneath*). Are you ready?

MARSHALL (*underneath*). Aaaah!

KAY (*underneath*). Are you ready?

MARSHALL (*underneath*). Aaaaaaaah!

(*A great scream from* MARSHALL)

FITZPATRICK (*underneath*). Okay. We're ready, Kay.

MARSHALL (*underneath*). Aaah. Get off!

KAY (*underneath*). Right. Glendenning. Have you got hold of a rope?

GLENDENNING (*underneath*). I ... I ... I ... I ... I've mmmm ... got one!

FITZPATRICK (*underneath*). It's not a rope he's got hold of, Mr Kay.

(*A burst of laughter from underneath*)

KAY (*underneath*). Are you right! Then pull together.

BENNETT (*underneath*). Pull together!

(*Another burst of laughter*)

KAY (*underneath*). Heave ... Heave ... Heave!

(FITZPATRICK *and* MARSHALL *pull together at one pole:* 'Heave! Heave! Heave!'

GLENDENNING *and* BENNETT *pull together at the second pole:* 'Heave! Heave! Heave!'

KAY *pulls alone at the nearest pole, one rope in either hand.*)

FITZPATRICK (*underneath*). Don't pull too hard, now, Glenny.

MARSHALL (*underneath*). You might do yourself an hurt.

(*They laugh, pulling up.*

Slowly the canvas is drawn up to the top of the poles and the men come into view.)

KAY. All right. Get in your side poles and tighten up your quarter guys.

(*The ropes are fastened off: threaded through holes in the pole for that purpose, then knotted, the men going to put in the side poles as they finish, hoisting up the edges of the tent.*)

MARSHALL. Rubber poles, Glenny. Make sure they bend. (*Demonstrates.*)

GLENDENNING. Aye!

> (GLENDENNING *laughs, fitting in the poles like everyone else.*
>
> FITZPATRICK *at one point, as he goes past, grabs* GLEN-DENNING's *backside, off-hand, whistling.*)

Aaaah!

BENNETT. Keep at it, Glenny.

MARSHALL. Never knew you were fond of animals, then, Bennett.

FITZPATRICK. Don't think he is, to tell the truth.

MARSHALL. Persecution.

FITZPATRICK. Persecution.

KAY. All right. All right. Just get 'em in.

FITZPATRICK. Get 'em in, there, Marshy.

MARSHALL. Get 'em in, I shall.

> (KAY *has started 'dressing-off' the ropes, i.e. wrapping them off, naval fashion, around the foot of the poles.*)

FITZPATRICK (*sings*). It's that man again ... It's that man again. (*Whispers urgently to* GLENDENNING.) Glenny! Glenny! Glenny!

> (*Gestures to* GLENDENNING: *approaching danger, trouble, watch it, careful ... burlesque. Whistles shrill, toneless tune.*
>
> EWBANK *has come in. Stands there, watching, intent.*)
> (*Sings drunkenly as he works.*) 'I was staggering home one night ... '

MARSHALL (*sings*). 'As sober as a newt ... '

FITZPATRICK. 'When I should see a sight
>   You'd think was rather cute ... '

> (MARSHALL *joins in the chorus.*)

MARSHALL. '*White* elephants, *pink* elephants,
>   Hanging on the wall ...

O ... oooo ... oh, what a palaver,
Fifty-one feet tall ... '

EWBANK (*to* BENNETT). That's not some bloody field you're
digging up. Just look at this here. Go steady, man! Go
steady! Kay! (*Presses in divot.*)

KAY. Right ... (*Dressing downstage pole*)

EWBANK (*to* MARSHALL). Walling. Walling! God Christ.
They stand about as if they were paying *you*!

KAY. Aye ... Walling.

EWBANK (*to* GLENDENNING). And look! Look! Look!
Look! Look! Look! Look! Look! Look! Don't walk
around as if you were at home. God damn and blast. Just
look at this ... !

GLENDENNING. I'm ... I'm ... I'm ... I'm ... I' m ...

EWBANK. That's all right, then.

(*The men have begun to hang the walling, hooking it up on
the rope that underlies and is sewn into the lower edge of the
canvas.*)

That's a nice bit of canvas, Kay.

KAY. It is. (*Nods, looking up at it.*)

EWBANK. They don't make them like that no more. (*Gestures
at tent.*) 'Least, not if I can help it. (*Laughs at his own
humour.*) It'd be too damn expensive.

KAY. Aye. It would.

EWBANK (*pleased, contemplating*). Would you believe it?

KAY. Aye?

EWBANK. It's the first time I've hired a bit of my own tenting.
It'll go down in the books you know. Pay meself with one
hand what I tek out with the other.

KAY. Aye! (*Laughs dutifully.*)

EWBANK. I'll never do it again. Never. Never have to.

KAY. No. Well. It's worth making a splash.

EWBANK. Splash? By God, this is a bloody thunderclap! It's
not just the tent I'm paying for. God, Christ. I wish it was.

No. No. (*To men*) Hang it! Hang it! Hang it! Hang it!
Hook it up! That's what they're there for. (*To* KAY) Three
or four hundred people here. Bloody string orchestra.
Waiters. Chef. I could buy four marquees with what I've
laid out here ... Ah, well. That's another matter. (*Looks
round, examining canvas.*) Let's hope it keeps fine. Have you
got the lining?

KAY. It's on the truck ...

EWBANK. No marks on it, Kay. And no marks on this either.
(*Indicates canvas.*) Four lasses, eh?

KAY. Aye ...

EWBANK. They'll cost you a packet. If I had four I'd set 'em
to work and retire. (*Laughs. Wanders round, examining.*)
Four. And I can't even manage one. And none of 'em
married?

KAY. No, no. They're still at school.

EWBANK. By God. If you had the benefit of my experience
you'd never set a lass at school. God Christ, they're only
good for one damn thing. And for that you don't have to
read a book.

KAY (*laughing*). Aye.

EWBANK. You've kept your eye on them relieving themselves,
have you?

KAY. Aye. They've been all right.

EWBANK. I don't give a damn myself. I've told you that
already. But I can't have the old lady looking out of the
window and not knowing where to put herself. (*To*
MARSHALL) Leave that side alone. You want it open to
bring the floor in. (*To* KAY) I noticed on the truck, Kay.
That floor costs a bloody fortune. When you put it on you
want to load it near the front. If a bit drops off it's done.
That's a lovely bit of sewing. (*Looking up*) Look at that
seam. (*Reads.*) 'Made by F. Ewbank to commemorate the
wedding of his daughter Claire.' My wife chose it.

KAY. The tent?

EWBANK. The bloody name. Paul. That's another of her choices ...

BENNETT. Shall we get the battens in, Kay?

KAY. Aye. Start fetching them in. And watch the walling.

(*The men, as they finish off the walling, leaving the one side open, go off to fetch in the battens which they begin to lay out on the floor.*

BENNETT *has raised the muslin ridges a few inches, fastening them off to enable the battens to go underneath. The ropes for raising these are threaded by* FITZPATRICK *and* BENNETT *before the canvas is raised*)

CLAIRE *has come in. Wanders round.* FITZPATRICK *whistles a tune.*)

EWBANK. Do you know how many tents we have out this week?

KAY. Quite a lot, I know.

EWBANK. Thirty-four. And that's just about the lot. If the wind gets under this we'll have some trouble. It blows like a bloody hurricane up here.

KAY. It's a lovely view.

EWBANK. Aye. It is. Whenever you can see it. At one time, do you know, there was nothing in that valley but a farm, a mill, and half a dozen houses. And what're you doing out here you wouldn't be better doing somewhere else?

(CLAIRE *has been wandering round the edges of the tent, looking around, slow ... only now has she been noticed by* EWBANK.)

CLAIRE. They're coming out to have a look. (*To* KAY) See how you're getting on.

EWBANK. We're all right. We don't need no helpers. (*Looks off.*)

CLAIRE (*to* KAY). Best to keep him on his toes.

KAY (*laughs*). Aye. (KAY *is dressing the second pole.*)

EWBANK. They don't need any supervision. Not with Kay. How long've you been with me? Three years. That's about as long as anybody in this place. They don't stay long. I employ anybody here, you know. Anybody who'll work. Miners who've coughed their lungs up, fitters who've lost their fingers, madmen who've run away from home. (*Laughs.*)

(*As the men go in and out they gaze over at* CLAIRE, FITZPATRICK *still whistling his tune whenever he appears.*) They don't mind. They know me. They can soon get shut. I've the biggest turnover of manual labour in this town. I take on all those that nobody else'll employ. See that? (*He indicates the inscription on the tent.*)

CLAIRE. You'll look well if we put it off.

EWBANK. Put it off? You'll not get this chance again. Not from me. Not from him either. (*He thumbs off, to* KAY.) She's marrying a bloody aristocrat, Kay. He's so refined if it wasn't for his britches he'd be invisible.

CLAIRE. Not like somebody else we know ...

EWBANK. Oh, she doesn't mind. Frank by name and frank by nature. If they don't like it they soon get shut. Have you ever seen a straight line, Bennett?

BENNETT. A straight line?

EWBANK. Well I have, man, and that's not one of them. (*He indicates the rows of battens they're laying across the floor.*) By ... ! Just look at this. Grass. Grass. Fitzpatrick!

FITZPATRICK. Yes, sir.

EWBANK. Don't bloody well sir me or I'll fetch you one round your ear. I'm not too old. Rest them ... *rest* them ... gently. (*To* KAY *and* CLAIRE) The trouble I take. What for? I might as well be shoving up a circus. (*Then, looking up at the tent*) I'm going to like this tent. Do you know? I'm going to like it, very much.

(PAUL *has come in and had a look around, hands in pockets.*)

PAUL (*to* EWBANK). Do you know. For one minute there, I thought I'd come in to find you working.

EWBANK. I am working.

PAUL. I heard you. From the house.

EWBANK. My work's done here. I'm a bloody artisan, I am. Not a worker. (*To* KAY) He's never believed that, Kay. And he's a ... Well, I don't know what he is. He's supposed to be summat.

PAUL (*to* KAY). I'm a drain on his pocket for one thing. He must have told you that.

EWBANK. Aye. For one thing. And as for another ... Aye, well. Least said, soonest mended. (*To* MARSHALL) Have you got that level? I don't want no ups and downs.

PAUL (*to* CLAIRE). How are you feeling?

CLAIRE. All right. (*Laughs.*)

PAUL. I don't know. (*Thumbs at* EWBANK *behind his back then looks up at the tent.*)

CLAIRE. It's going to be very nice.

PAUL. Lovely.

CLAIRE (*gesturing at tent*). Why, what's the matter with it?

PAUL. Nothing.

CLAIRE. Nothing.

PAUL (*broadly*). We don't get married every day.

CLAIRE. Let's all thank God for that.

PAUL (*to* KAY). I'll give you a hand if you like.

KAY. Well, I don't know ...

PAUL (*broadly*). I've done it before. I know a bit about it. (*Gestures at* EWBANK.) When I was younger he used to let me help him, for half a crown an hour. Did the work of three men. Quite a saving.

KAY. I reckon it must have been at that.

PAUL. Well, then. Let's set about it.

(*He goes, joining the men fetching in the battens.*)

EWBANK (*to* KAY). I'm off in. I'll leave you to it before the rest of 'em arrive. (*Gestures at house.*) Is there ought you want while I'm at it?

KAY. No, no. We'll be all right.

EWBANK (*to* CLAIRE). Working under t'boss's eye. They none of them like it.

CLAIRE. That's going to be the floor, then.

EWBANK. That's right. This time tomorrow you'll be dancing over it light as a feather.

CLAIRE. Let's hope you're right.

EWBANK. Nay, damn it all. I wish I had my time over again, I do. (*To* KAY) I'm off in, then. (*To* CLAIRE) Are you coming with me?

CLAIRE. I think I better.

EWBANK (*to* KAY). Here, come with me, lad. I'll show you what I mean with that bloody load ... (*Going*)

> (KAY *glances round then follows* EWBANK *who goes out with his arm absent-mindedly round* CLAIRE'*s shoulders.*
> PAUL *has come in with his battens: he's followed by* GLENDENNING, *laying them side by side.*)

PAUL (*to* GLENDENNING). What's your name, then?

GLENDENNING. G ... G ... G ... G ... Glenny!

FITZPATRICK. That's Glenny.

MARSHALL. He's a bit soft in the head.

GLENDENNING. I ... I ... I ... I ... Aye. I am. (*He laughs.*)

BENNETT. Takes all sorts to make a world.

PAUL. That's right. It does. What do you think of this one, then? (*Indicates tent.*)

> (BENNETT *has started to bring in the sections of polished floor, beginning to lay them on the battens.*)

FITZPATRICK. A bit of all right, boy.

MARSHALL. Your old man can make a tent when he wants to.

PAUL. That's right. He can.

FITZPATRICK. There's not many of them around these days.

PAUL. What's that?

FITZPATRICK. Butterflies with caps on.

(*They laugh.*)

PAUL (*to* GLENDENNING). Will you give us a lift with that?

GLENDENNING. Aye. Aye! I will.

PAUL. Do you like working here, Glenny?

GLENDENNING. I ... I ... I ... Aye!

PAUL. Yes?

GLENDENNING. Aye ... I ... I ... I ...

MARSHALL (*sings*). Aye, yi, yi, yi ... Aye, yi, yi, yi ...

GLENDENNING. I ... I ... I couldn't nnnnnn ... get a job anywhere else.

PAUL. There's not many places.

GLENDENNING. They w ... w ... w ... won't have you if you're o ... o ... off your head.

PAUL. Are you off your head?

GLENDENNING. Aye! (*Laughs pleasantly.*)

FITZPATRICK. You'd never have believed it.

(*They laugh.*)

GLENDENNING (*to* PAUL). W ... w ... w ... what do you d ... d ... d ... do, then?

PAUL. Me?

GLENDENNING. F ... f ... f ... for a living.

PAUL. Well, I'm a sort of a ... No, no. I'm a kind of ... I don't do anything at all as a matter of fact.

GLENDENNING. Oh, aye!

PAUL. You fancy a bit of that, do you?

GLENDENNING. Aye! (*Laughs.*)

(MAURICE *comes in.*)

PAUL. Ah, well, Glenny. Each one to his trade.

GLENDENNING. I ... I ... I ... I ... I'd like to give it a g... g ... g ... go, though! (*Laughs.*)

41

PAUL. Aye, well. That's a privilege few of us can afford, Glenny.

(MAURICE *has come in while they're working, wandering round until he comes to* PAUL.

MAURICE *wears a jacket and flannels, a bit crumpled. He's tall, perhaps with a moustache: fairly ordinary and straight-forward.*)

FITZPATRICK. Can we do anything then, to help?

MAURICE. Oh, I belong here as well. (*To* PAUL, *casual*) I though I better warn you. There's your Grandad on his way.

PAUL (*carrying on working*). Aye. (*He's bringing in and laying sections of polished floor.*)

MAURICE. Have you seen her anywhere around?

PAUL. She was here just now. A few minutes ago.

MAURICE. This is where all the do-dah's going to be?

PAUL. Seems so.

MAURICE. I can't see why we couldn't have had it in the house.

PAUL. He says there wasn't room.

MAURICE. There seems plenty room to me.

PAUL. You know Frank.

MAURICE. By name and nature.

(*They laugh.*)

I suppose it means a lot to him.

PAUL. A bit of his own tenting over his head.

MAURICE. I suppose it does. You haven't got a fag, have you?

PAUL. I'm working. (*To* MARSHALL) Have you got a fag to spare?

MARSHALL. Me? No. Never. (*Scandalized, he turns to* BENNETT.)

BENNETT (*instant*). No. Not one at all.

FITZPATRICK. Here. Have one of mine.

PAUL. This's the blushing bridegroom.

FITZPATRICK. I thought as much.

MAURICE (*lights up from* FITZPATRICK). I'll fetch you one out of the house if you'll hang on.

FITZPATRICK. S'all right. Just put it on me wages.

(*They laugh.*)

MAURICE. Good God. (*Coughs.*)

FITZPATRICK. S'all right. I make them up meself. Good Irish baccy, there is, wrapped up in that.

MARSHALL. Swept up, that is, from some of the best bar-rooms in the town.

(*They laugh, still working.*)

FITZPATRICK. No, no, now. He's having you on.

MAURICE. Let's hope you're right. (*To* PAUL) If I didn't feel so exhausted I'd have given you a hand.

PAUL. I know the feeling.

MAURICE. I don't know. What are we supposed to do in here, for instance?

PAUL (*shrugs*). Dance around. Look jolly.

MAURICE (*surreptitiously putting out cigarette*). It's a lot of fuss.

PAUL. It may never happen again. You might be lucky.

MAURICE. Aye. Let's hope you're right ... What's the matter with him?

(*While they've been talking,* GLENDENNING *has gone out and returned carrying his fourteen-pound sledgehammer, proudly, over his shoulder.*

Now, smiling, he marches up and down for PAUL'*s benefit.*)

PAUL. He's a ... Well done, Glenny.

GLENDENNING (*pleased*). Aye!

(KAY *has returned, with him are* OLD EWBANK *and* OLD MRS EWBANK, *in her sixties, a small, practical, homely person.*)

OLD MRS E. (*to* KAY). If we're in the way just let us know ...

KAY. No, no. It's all right by me.

FITZPATRICK (*calling to* GLENDENNING). Hup, two, three, four ... Right a ... a ... a ... a ... about—*turn!* By God. They ought to make him a bloody general.

OLD MRS E. You're having a look as well, Maurice?

MAURICE. Surveying the scene of battle.

OLD MRS E. Oh, now. Get on.

MAURICE. Best to take precautions.

(PAUL *drifts back to work.*)

OLD MRS E. We're having a struggle—now he's seen the tent—to keep him retired. (*Indicating* OLD EWBANK *whose arm she holds*)

OLD EWBANK. What?

OLD MRS E. (*shouting*). We have a struggle keeping you retired.

OLD EWBANK (*to* MAURICE). Good God. I am. We've never had this damn fuss before.

OLD MRS E. It'll sink in, don't worry.

FITZPATRICK (*in background*). Hup, two, three, four ... Hup, two, three, four ... Lee ... eeeeft wheeee—eeeeeeel!

KAY. Glendenning, for Christ's sake. Put that hammer down.

MARSHALL. You want to watch how you speak to him, Kay. Or he'll fetch you one with that right over the head. (*Nudges* PAUL.)

KAY (*to* GLENDENNING). Come on. Come on, now. Let's have this floor down.

(*Gently,* KAY *takes the hammer from him. Smiling, pleased,* GLENDENNING *joins the others.*)

FITZPATRICK. The army's the place for you, Glenny, all right.

MARSHALL. Frighten the bloody enemy to death.

(OLD EWBANK *has crossed to* BENNETT, *who is working assiduously at the floor, and continues to do so.*)

OLD EWBANK. You know what I used to be?

BENNETT. What? (*Looks up startled.*)

44

OLD EWBANK. Rope-maker. (*Pauses for effect.*) You see all the ropes that hold up this tent?

BENNETT. What? Aye ... (*Looks up.*)

OLD EWBANK. I made 'em!

BENNETT. That's very good.

OLD EWBANK. No. No. Not for good. The ones I made're all worn out. Started making tents in my old age. Passed it on.

BENNETT (*working*). Ah. Yes.

OLD EWBANK. You haven't seen the old man?

BENNETT. Old man?

OLD EWBANK. The gaffer. (*Waits for* BENNETT *to nod, mystified.*) That's my son. He owns all this now. He made it.

BENNETT. Aye?

OLD EWBANK. The tent.

BENNETT. Aye ...

OLD EWBANK (*suddenly*). Ropes. That's my trade. Nowt like it.

PAUL (*calling*). I should get him out of here, Gran. Something's likely to fall on his head.

(*A section of floor, in fact, has narrowly missed* OLD EWBANK's *head.*)

OLD MRS E. I will. I will ... I never knew you were employed here, Paul.

PAUL. I don't know ... Got to find your natural level, Gran.

OLD MRS E. I've heard that before, I think, somewhere else —

PAUL. Aye. I believe you have. (*Laughs.*)

OLD EWBANK (*to* BENNETT). The best education money can buy. That's my grandson. Oxford. Cambridge. University College. All the rest. Ask him about anything and he'll come up with an answer.

BENNETT. Oh. Aye ...

OLD EWBANK. Not got his father's skill.

FITZPATRICK (*joining in*). No?

OLD EWBANK. Sure? I am. He couldn't thread a needle. Have you seen the way that canvas is cut? (*To* OLD MRS EWBANK) ... What is it?

KAY. Come on, Fitzpatrick. Let's see you stuck in.

OLD EWBANK. I've come up for the wedding. Otherwise I wouldn't be here.

BENNETT. Ah, yes.

OLD MRS E. (*to* OLD EWBANK). It'll soon be time for dinner.

OLD EWBANK. I'll what?

OLD MRS E. (*shouting*). Dinner.

OLD EWBANK. Good God, we've only just got up.

(*They go out slowly,* OLD MRS EWBANK *taking his arm.*)

FITZPATRICK. A fine old man.

MARSHALL. One of the great old-timers.

BENNETT (*to* PAUL). He has a very high opinion of yourself.

PAUL. Has he? I know the thing you mean.

(*They laugh.*)

MAURICE (*to* PAUL). I'll be off, then. See you in the house.

(MAURICE *goes.*)

Thanks for the cigarette.

FITZPATRICK. Not at all. (*To* PAUL) A college man.

PAUL. Yes?

FITZPATRICK. Yourself. I could see it at a glance.

PAUL. Well, then. That's pretty good.

FITZPATRICK. I've always fancied that, you know, myself. Books. Study. A pile of muffins by the fire.

MARSHALL. A pile of what?

(*They laugh.*)

FITZPATRICK. And the bridegroom feller. The one that's such a great one with the cigarettes.

(*They laugh.*)

PAUL. A doctor.

FITZPATRICK. A doctor! By God.

MARSHALL. Fitzie's always fancied himself as that.

FITZPATRICK. Aye. The stethoscope is my natural weapon. There's not many a thing, now, that I couldn't find with that.

(*They laugh.*
Most of the floor is now in, though GLENDENNING *and* KAY *could still be bringing in the last,* BENNETT, MARSHALL, FITZPATRICK *and* PAUL *going round fitting the polished sections into place, on top of the battens.*)

And your sister's been a nurse?

PAUL. That's right.

FITZPATRICK. Ah, yes. A hospital, now. You can't go wrong with that.

PAUL. And yourself?

FITZPATRICK. Me? Why, I'm like the rest of them.

MARSHALL. An honest working-man.

FITZPATRICK. That's right.

MARSHALL. Born and bred in Ireland!

FITZPATRICK. Like every one before me.

PAUL. And ... (*Indicating* MARSHALL)

MARSHALL. Marshall.

FITZPATRICK. It's the funniest Irish name I've ever heard.

MARSHALL. My mother was a decent Irish woman.

FITZPATRICK. That's not what she told him, now, when she met his grand old man.

(*They laugh.*)

BENNETT (*at a gesture from* PAUL). Oh, I'm good old English stock.

MARSHALL. Stock, did he say?

FITZPATRICK. English born, English bred:

　　　　　Long in the leg, and thick in the head.

(*They laugh.*)

47

BENNETT. Done a bit of everything.

MARSHALL. He has. And everybody, too.

> (*They laugh.*)

BENNETT. And I end up in a place like this.

PAUL. Why's that?

BENNETT. I don't know.

MARSHALL. He likes the fresh air: coming through the windows.

BENNETT. Fresh air. (*Laughs.*) You get fresh air all right, inside that cab.

MARSHALL. Empire-builders! That's us!

> (*They laugh.*
> *The floor now is laid, smooth squares of parquet that slot together over the battens.*
> *The men pause, resting.*)

BENNETT (*tousles* GLENDENNING's *hair*). How's old Glenny? He's the only one of us that doesn't hold a grudge.

GLENDENNING. Ay ... ay ... Aye! (*Laughs.*)

BENNETT. Glass hammers and rubber nails. All day long. Never remembers.

MARSHALL. Does it in his sleep I shouldn't wonder.

GLENDENNING. I ... I ... I ... Aye! I do!

MARSHALL. Nearly caught him this morning sticking stakes in your dad's green grass.

FITZPATRICK. Aye. We did. That'd have put the kibosh on it, Glenny!

BENNETT. He's a good lad at knocking in stakes. You should see him with that hammer, Isn't that right, Glenny?

GLENDENNING. Aye! (*Laughs.*)

MARSHALL. Hits it once in every four.

FITZPATRICK. Damn great pit you find, with a little stake sticking up inside.

BENNETT. He's a good lad.

KAY (*coming back*). Have you finished off that flooring? Bennett. Fitzpatrick. Can you carry in the lining?

FITZPATRICK. Nay, steady on, Kay. We've had no snap for hours.

KAY (*getting watch out*). Get the lining in, then you can have it. Best get it under cover, then we'll be all right.

FITZPATRICK. Ah, come on, Glenny ...

MARSHALL. And where's he been the last half hour?

FITZPATRICK. Tipping it back, no doubt, with number one ... (*Mimes drinking.*)

(*They laugh.* KAY *takes no notice.*)

KAY. Marshall. Come on. Let's have you ... (*As* PAUL *makes to follow*) There's your mother looking for you outside ...

(*From outside come* FITZPATRICK, MARSHALL, *etc.,* *saying, 'Morning ... Good morning', and* MRS EWBANK's *pleasant reply, 'Morning ... '*

MRS EWBANK *comes in as men leave: a pleasant, practical-looking woman in her middle forties, not smart but certainly not dowdy.*)

PAUL. We were just fetching in the lining ...

MRS EWBANK (*looking round*). I thought I'd just pop out ... Don't worry. I won't get in the way. It's not often I see one of your father's tents go up.

PAUL. No ... I suppose not.

MRS EWBANK. It's going to look very grand.

PAUL. So they say.

MRS EWBANK. How have they been getting on? (*Indicating the men who've gone outside*)

PAUL. All right.

MRS EWBANK. This wood ... (*Walking over the floor*) A few years back one man got a splinter in his hand, left it unattended ...

PAUL. Turned septic ...

MRS EWBANK (*looks up*). He had to have one of his fingers off.

PAUL. Dangerous job.

MRS EWBANK. Yes.

> (*She walks on after a moment, looking round. Sees inscription overhead, on the canvas.*)

I didn't know he'd written that.

PAUL. All done by stencils.

MRS EWBANK. Is that it? (*Gazes up at it.*)

PAUL. Takes it all to heart.

MRS EWBANK. Yes. He does. (*Pause*). Why? Don't you like it? (*Casual, pleasant*)

PAUL. I don't know. (*Shrugs, laughs.*) I suppose I do ... Frank by name ... (*Imitates EWBANK's voice.*)

MRS EWBANK. But not by nature.

PAUL. No?

MRS EWBANK. No.

> (*From outside come the voices of the men.*)

FITZPATRICK (*off*). To you ... (*Sing-song*)

MARSHALL (*off*). To me ...

FITZPATRICK (*off*). From me ...

MARSHALL (*off*). From you ...

FITZPATRICK (*off*). Here you are, Glenny ... Ooooops!

> (*Laughter off.*)

MRS EWBANK. Is there anything we can get them?

PAUL. Probably a pot of tea would go down very well.

> (*Pause.*)

MRS EWBANK. Are you going off, then?

PAUL. Off?

MRS EWBANK. When all this is over.

PAUL. Suppose so.

MRS EWBANK. Where to?

PAUL. Don't know ...

> (*Pause.*)

MRS EWBANK. Suppose you'll let us know.

PAUL. Yep.

MRS EWBANK. Well, then ... I'll see about the tea.

PAUL. Don't worry ... (*Holds up his hands.*)

MRS EWBANK. No, no. (*She smiles.*)

    (*She goes out as the men come in, bringing three bags of muslin with them.*)

FITZPATRICK (*off*). I knew a man called Glenny

        Who went to spend a penny:

        He got inside,

        And tried and tried –

        But found he hadn't any. (*Entering*)

    (*The men burst into laughter, putting down the bags, GLENDENNING smiling, pleased.*)

MARSHALL. There was a man Fitzpatrick ...

FITZPATRICK. He wouldn't know a poem if he saw one.

MARSHALL. Who sat on an egg to hatch it:

        He sat and sat,

BENNETT. And sh ... at and sh ... at.

MARSHALL. But found he hadn't cracked it.

    (*They laugh amongst themselves, KAY coming in last.*)

KAY. Right, then ... You can break it up.

FITZPATRICK (*to PAUL*). Kay, you know, is a very conscientious man. Always does as he's told. Keeps strictly to instructions.

KAY. It's a damn good job there's somebody here to do something.

    (*They're going.*)

MARSHALL. It's right. It's right. Value for money is his motto.

FITZPATRICK (*arm round GLENDENNING as they go*). Grub at last, Glenny.

GLENDENNING. Aye!

FITZPATRICK (*winking to PAUL*). You'll see the bloody sparks fly now.

(*They go, leaving* PAUL *alone.*
Their laughter and shouts fade outside.)
(*off*). Here, Glenny. Have a snap at that!
(*Laughter.*
It grows silent.
PAUL *stands gazing round at the interior, grows abstracted.*
Sits on bag of muslin, arms resting on knees.
Begins to whistle quietly to himself: a slow, rather melancholy tune.
After a while lights slowly fade.)

END OF ACT ONE

ACT TWO

The muslin is being taped to the muslin ridges which have been raised to shoulder height. Most of the muslin now has been taped, and most of it has been laced — in the same manner as the canvas before it.

The men work minus GLENDENNING *and* KAY.

FITZPATRICK. Do you know. I never fasten one of these without thinking of my mother.

(MARSHALL *and* BENNETT *laugh*.)

MARSHALL. Why's that, Fitzie?

FITZPATRICK. I don't know. I don't know. I'd go a long way, now, to find that out.

(KAY *has come in*.)

KAY. All right, then. Let's have it out.

FITZPATRICK. Out?

MARSHALL. Out.

FITZPATRICK. Out we shall.

(*They draw the muslin out on either side: a thin drape in green, yellow and white, each band of colour is perhaps two feet or eighteen inches in width: the seams are ruched.*

There are three pieces in all, corresponding to the three pieces of canvas: one piece between each of the three poles (1 and 2) and the end piece (3) at the back of the stage.

Having laid it out across the floor the men go back to complete the lacing.)

MARSHALL (*looking round*). Where's Glenny, then? He's taking a long time to take them cups back.

FITZPATRICK. When you give Glenny a job he likes, he gives it his full attention.

(*They laugh.*)

KAY. I wish I could say the same for yourself. Now get on with your lacing.

(FITZPATRICK *glances at* MARSHALL. *They laugh.*)

MARSHALL. Kay. It's lovely stuff. It is. It is ... Made too, if I'm not mistaken, specially for the occasion.

FITZPATRICK. I remember the first day I came here, now, to work. At the beginning of the summer.

MARSHALL (*looking at the sky*). It's damn near the end of it now.

FITZPATRICK. Except in the army, I'd never seen a tent before.

BENNETT. Aye!

FITZPATRICK. We were driven out of the town, on one of the trucks ... Up the valley, past a lot of trees and hills. And suddenly ... looking down ... this field. Full of tents. White canvas, everywhere you looked.

MARSHALL. Big as a balloon.

FITZPATRICK. Big as an elephant ... Aye.

(*They work for a moment in silence. Then:*)

When we got down here, and we got out of the cab ...

MARSHALL. One of the favourites ... Not riding on the back.

FITZPATRICK. I stood there, looking up at them and thinking, 'It's a damn great pity it is, to take them down at all.'

MARSHALL. I remember that day very well. Almost four hours before he did a stroke of work himself.

(*They laugh.*)

KAY. Fitzpatrick, get on with your bloody lacing.

(MARSHALL *and* FITZPATRICK *exchange glances, then laugh.*)

MARSHALL. Four daughters!

(*They laugh.*

FITZPATRICK *has begun to sing as he works.*)

MARSHALL. Where were you working, then, Kay, before you came to Ewbank's?

KAY. I was working.

BENNETT. Kay was in the nick. Isn't that right?

(KAY *doesn't answer.*)

MARSHALL. Well, I never knew that. Is that right, then?

BENNETT. It is.

(FITZPATRICK *stops singing.*)

FITZPATRICK. In the lock-up, Kay, were you?

(KAY *doesn't answer but continues lacing.*)

MARSHALL. And what was he in for? If that's not the wrong thing to ask.

BENNETT. I don't know. You better ask him.

(MARSHALL *laughs.*)

FITZPATRICK. Come on, now, Kay. What did they put you in for?

KAY. Get on with your lacing.

MARSHALL. Ah, come on, now, Kay. Aren't you going to give us a clue?

FITZPATRICK. Was it animal, vegetable, or mineral?

(*They laugh.*)

KAY. I was sent up ...

MARSHALL. Aye?

KAY. For not minding my own business. (*Factual: goes on working without being distracted.*)

FITZPATRICK. Is that a fact? (*To the others*) God damn it: we deserve to be put inside an' all.

(*They laugh.*)

MARSHALL. Kay ... you ... me ... Glenny.

(*Following* KAY's *lead, they hook the corners and quarters of the muslin up, in the same fashion as the canvas was first raised on the 'quarter' and corner side poles. It hangs in a great loop now across the flooring.*)

FITZPATRICK. Ah, it's a great life if you can afford it.

MARSHALL. And what, now, is that?

FITZPATRICK. A wife ... home ... children.

MARSHALL. Hot chocolate.

FITZPATRICK. Hot chocolate.

MARSHALL. Toes ...

FITZPATRICK. Toes ...

MARSHALL. Fingers.

FITZPATRICK. Fingers.

KAY. All right, then ... Let's have it up.

> (*The men have scrambled underneath, the muslin billowing as they reach the ropes.*)

Are you ready?

BENNETT. Ready ...

MARSHALL. Ready, Mr Kay.

FITZPATRICK. Ready, Mr Kay; you're right.

> (*They laugh.*)

KAY. Right, then ... together.

> (*They haul up the muslin, fastening it off.*)

MARSHALL. *Christopher!* Just look at that!

> (GLENDENNING *has come in, looking pleased, standing to one side and eating, so that they all might see, a very large bun.*
>
> *As they turn to look across he smiles dazedly at them, eating.*)

FITZPATRICK. Eating on the job, Mr Kay! Mr Kay! Glendenning here is eating a big fat bun.

BENNETT. Did you nick it from the house, Glenny?

GLENDENNING. No ... n ... n ... no. (*He shakes his head.*)

FITZPATRICK. Then where ... then what ... then what*ever* have you done with ours, Glenny?

> (GLENDENNING *happily shakes his head.*)

MARSHALL. He's eaten it!

> (GLENDENNING, *happy, dazed, smiling, still eating, shakes his head again.*)

BENNETT. I don't understand, Glenny. Do you mean to say, the lady of the house ...

MARSHALL. Herself ...

BENNETT. Gave you a bun? And didn't give us one — as well?

GLENDENNING. I ... I ... I ... Aye! (*Nods happily, putting the last large fragment into his mouth.*)

> (*The men start taping up the muslin to the sides of the tent. It's hung in such a way that it hangs slightly, billowing in, a soft lining to the tent.*)

FITZPATRICK. Well, I'll be damned. I will.

> (GLENDENNING *nods at them, smiling.*)

MARSHALL. And not a bite to share between us.

KAY. Glendenning, make yourself useful. Pick up the bags.

> (GLENDENNING *still gazes at them, smiling.*)

Glendenning. Have you heard?

GLENDENNING. Aye! (*Happily goes to work.*)

FITZPATRICK. Well, I'll be damned. I *will* be damned. All this time I've been thinking: Glenny is a friend of mine. If I have *one* friend in this big wide world, it's Glenny. All the rest I can do without.

GLENDENNING. I ... I ... I ... Aye!

MARSHALL. It's a great and terrible disappointment. I shall never get over this. I shan't.

> (MARSHALL *gets out his handkerchief, dabs his eyes, wipes his nose ...*)

FITZPATRICK. Aye. This really is the end. For sure.

KAY. Keep your folds even. Space it out. Space it.

MARSHALL. Work your fingers to the bone. Break your back. Crack your head. And out there, all the time, Glenny is cramming his face with buns. It's more than anyone could stand.

> (GLENDENNING *is pleased with all this, no more so than with* MARSHALL's *attempts at crying: he watches, smiling, anxious for them to go on.*)

KAY (*going*). Bennett ... Give me a hand in with the furniture.

BENNETT. I think Kay's greatest disappointment in life—
prison sentence apart—is for him not to see me working—
hard.

(BENNETT *follows Kay out.*

FITZPATRICK *signals* MARSHALL.)

FITZPATRICK. By God, and I could have done with that
bun, Marshy. My stomach's trembling here from lack of
food.

GLENDENNING (*laughing*). Aye!

MARSHALL. When I get a bun myself—*which I shall*—not a
crumb of it will I give away.

FITZPATRICK. No, no. Not a drop.

MARSHALL. At least, not to a *certain person* whom I shall not
go to the trouble of puttin' a name.

(KAY *and* BENNETT *come back in carrying white metalwork chairs and tables.*)

FITZPATRICK. No, no. That's a fact.

MARSHALL. The one I have in mind has cream on.

KAY (*to* BENNETT). Come on. Let's have some more inside.

BENNETT. Bloody hell ... (*Groans to himself.*)

(KAY *and* BENNETT *go out.*)

FITZPATRICK. With a strawberry on top.

MARSHALL. And thick jam inside.

FITZPATRICK. With a touch of apricot.

MARSHALL. About as big as a Christmas pud. (*Shapes it.*)

(GLENDENNING, *as he listens, loses his smile. For a while
he watches them concernedly then, slowly, he turns away.*)

FITZPATRICK. Aye. Aye. I know just the shop. They sell
them by the score. God, it takes half an hour to get through
one of them.

MARSHALL. And that, mind you, is just the start.

FITZPATRICK. Aye. Aye. The rate we work, the money we
earn, we s'll have enough for half a dozen.

MARSHALL. I can just see it, sitting there. Waiting to be eaten up.

BENNETT (*coming in with* KAY, *with another table*). Oh, now you're not letting them get on top? (*To* GLENDENNING)
(GLENDENNING *is still turned away, slowly picking pieces up.*)

MARSHALL. Ah, Fitzie, now. Just look.

FITZPATRICK. He's ... Why? ... (*Stepping round so that he can look in* GLENDENNING'*s face*) You're not wishing, now, that you'd given us a bit of that?
(KAY *and* BENNETT *go out again.*)

MARSHALL. He's wishing now he'd broken off a bit. Perhaps, even, as much as half.

FITZPATRICK. Or more.

MARSHALL. Or more. Come on, now, Glenny ... I was pulling your leg.
(GLENDENNING *is immobilized, standing now with his head hanging down.*)

FITZPATRICK. Why, you've gone and made the feller roar.

MARSHALL. I have?

FITZPATRICK. There are tears streaming from his eyes.

MARSHALL. And nose.

FITZPATRICK. And nose.

BENNETT (*carrying in a tin of polish and rag*). You want to leave the lad alone.
(GLENDENNING *has begun to shake his head slightly, turned away, wiping his eyes and sobbing.*)

KAY (*coming in with another table*). Look out. Look out. He's here.

FITZPATRICK. Kay is ever such a conscientious feller. It just shows the benefits, now, of being put inside. (*Going*)
(*They laugh.*
FITZPATRICK *goes.*)

BENNETT (*crossing to* GLENDENNING). Ah, now, Glenny. Don't take it so much to heart.

> (GLENDENNING *shakes his head. He goes.*
>
> MARSHALL *laughs.*)

You want to leave him alone!

MARSHALL. Jump on your bloody head. (*Faces up to him, then darts away, laughing.*)

> (EWBANK *has come in behind them, watching them.*)

EWBANK. *Get your boots off that bloody floor!* God Christ. Just look at him. Studs and half a ton of earth sliding about on top of it.

> (BENNETT *is standing at the centre of the polished floor.*)

Get your boots off, off, off, off, off, off, if you're going to stand on it.

KAY. Bennett. We'll work this side. You work that. (*Indicating* BENNETT *should take his boots off*)

BENNETT. Me?

> (*It's evident, though not too much, that* EWBANK *has had a drop.*)

MARSHALL. His socks are full of holes, Kay.

FITZPATRICK (*entering with polish*). He hasn't got no socks.

> (*They laugh, starting to polish.*)

MARSHALL. If he takes his boots off in here there'll not be one of us left alive.

EWBANK (*swaying slightly*). I take it that that lining's not been hung right yet.

KAY. No. No.

BENNETT. Bloody hell ... (*He's begun to take his boots off, sitting on the polished floor.*)

> (FITZPATRICK *has begun to sing, drunkenly.* GLENDENNING *has come back in.*)

FITZPATRICK. We hash a good night to ... night ...

MARSHALL. We'll have a good one to ... morrow ...

FITZPATRICK. We hash a few drops to ... night ...

MARSHALL. We'll have a few more to ... morrow ...

EWBANK (*head craning back*). Aye. That's going to look very nice.

(EWBANK *has become aware of* GLENDENNING, *walking, drooped, at a snail's pace.*)

KAY. They've been having him on ...

EWBANK. Ay, ay, ay ... Do you hear that, now. Do you hear?

FITZPATRICK. Aye. Aye. (*Ruffling* GLENDENNING'*s hair*) You're all right, aren't you?

EWBANK. I'm not having you tormenting that lad. A bloody half-wit. You ought to have more common sense.

MARSHALL. Aye. Aye. We should.

EWBANK (*has tripped up*). God damn and blast ... Glendenning. Give me a hand with this. (*Picks up the bag he's tripped over.*)

KAY. What's the *matter* with Fitzpatrick?

(FITZPATRICK *is doubled up, laughing.*)

MARSHALL. It's the smell. Bennett, for God's sake.

BENNETT. My feet are all right.

KAY. What?

BENNETT. I wash them. Every night.

MARSHALL. Soap and water.

FITZPATRICK. Soap and water.

(EWBANK *has sent* GLENDENNING *out.*)

MARSHALL. You could make a collander of his socks. Just look at them. Bennett, don't you have a wife?

KAY (*to* FITZPATRICK). If you find it so damn funny no doubt you'll tolerate your own.

MARSHALL. No. No. Don't ask him that. I'd rather be annihilated by Bennett than by Fitzpatrick. (*Looks up to the sky.*) If it has to come, O Lord, let it not be at the feet of my friend, Fitzpatrick.

EWBANK. Just watch that floor. Watch it. It's a precious thing

61

is that. (*To* KAY) I've sent Glendenning down to the shop.

FITZPATRICK (*to* MARSHALL, *polishing*). I hope, not for another tot.

EWBANK. What's that?

FITZPATRICK. I say: he's about the only decent one we've got.

MARSHALL. I hope to God it's nothing lethal: matches or a packet of cigarettes.

(MARSHALL *and* FITZPATRICK *laugh, polishing.*)

EWBANK. Have you levelled off that floor?

BENNETT. We have.

(MARSHALL *and* FITZPATRICK *have begun to sing the drinking song in quiet voices.*)

PAUL. I've had me snap. I've had me rest. Now. Where would you like me?

(PAUL *has come in, in shirt-sleeves hanging loosely down, his hands deep in his pockets, standing in the door, stooping slightly.*)

EWBANK (*looking up*). There's nowt in here for you, lad.

PAUL. I don't mind. I'll give a hand.

EWBANK. There's no need.

PAUL. No, no. I understand. Nevertheless ... I'll do whatever it is I'm able.

(*He goes to dress the muslin ropes on the main poles.*)

EWBANK. Marshall. Fetch in the walling. You can start hanging that.

(MARSHALL *gets up and goes out.*)

(*To* KAY) Keep that evenly spaced there, Kay.

KAY. Aye. We'll have it straight. Don't worry. (*Arranging muslin*)

(EWBANK *stands gazing round, a little helpless.*)

EWBANK. Aye, well ... (*looks at his watch*). I'll look in again in a few minutes. I shan't be long.

(EWBANK *goes.*

MARSHALL *comes in with the sack containing the muslin walling.*)

BENNETT (*working with his back to the door*). Has he gone?

MARSHALL. You can breathe again, feller. (*To* PAUL) No disrespect, mind, to you at all.

PAUL. No. No. None at all.

FITZPATRICK. What're you going to be at the wedding, then?

PAUL. Oh, I don't know ...

FITZPATRICK (*cheerful*). Not the best man, then?

PAUL. I might well be that.

(*They laugh.*)

FITZPATRICK. What did you study at the school, then?

PAUL. Nothing much.

MARSHALL. Nothing much, to God. You better not tell him that. (*Gestures at house.*)

(*They laugh.*

MARSHALL *has got out the muslin walling and starts to hang it.*)

FITZPATRICK (*loud*). I've always fancied myself, you know, as a criminal lawyer ...

MARSHALL. He's very good at that. Knows it from the inside ...

(*They laugh.*)

FITZPATRICK. No, no. I'm too old now, to go to school, and too damn poor to bother.

MARSHALL. But then, you know ... Talking of criminality ...

FITZPATRICK. That's right ...

MARSHALL (*to* PAUL). You were probably not aware that you were working in the presence of one such man himself.

FITZPATRICK. You are. I bet you didn't know it.

MARSHALL. A fair-minded, decent feller like yourself, coming in here, hoping to find himself amongst his equals.

Only to discover, behind his back, that one of *them* had crept in unnoticed.

PAUL (*laughing*).And who's that?

FITZPATRICK. Why, none other than—himself. (*Gestures at* KAY.)

BENNETT. I wish you'd pay a bit more attention to this here. Just look at the bloody floor. (*Polishing*)

FITZPATRICK. Attention, now. Attention.

KAY (*to* BENNETT). Watch that walling ... Fitzpatrick. I hope you're going to rub that floor.

(KAY *goes to dress one of the remaining muslin ropes.*)

BENNETT. Oh, God. My bloody back. (*To* PAUL) Have you ever suffered from rheumatism?

PAUL. I don't think I have.

BENNETT. One of the worst diseases known to man.

FITZPATRICK. Bloody indolence, more likely.

BENNETT. What's that?

FITZPATRICK. I say, you get it all the time.

BENNETT. I do. (*Holds his back, groans.*) God.

FITZPATRICK (*to* PAUL). On the other hand, what we haven't discovered—and speaking purely as a man familiar with nothing but his own profession—

(MARSHALL *snorts.*)

is, what crime this person, this man, who has inveigled himself into our presence, what crime it is, precisely, that he's committed.

MARSHALL. I hope it was nothing indecent to do with little girls.

FITZPATRICK. Good God. Crimes of that nature I cannot stand.

MARSHALL. I can't bear to read a word about them in the papers.

FITZPATRICK. I sincerely hope—I sincerely hope, Marshall— that it's nothing I'd be afraid to mention to me mother.

(*They laugh.*)

Come on, now, Kay. Between these four walls—or three and a half to be exact—what manner of crime was it that you committed? Were you driven to it by the pressures of the world; or is it simply that you're a rotten *sod*?

(*They laugh.*)

Kay is a very hard man. You'll get nothing out of him. He didn't suffer all that, you know, in vain. (*Friendly*) Isn't that right, Kay?

(KAY, *unmoved until now, has gone on with his work, not even looking up.*

Now, however, he pauses. He looks up very slowly. Then:)

KAY. And what sort of suffering have you done, Fitzpatrick?

FITZPATRICK. Suffering? By God. I'm suffering every day.

(MARSHALL *laughs, snorting.*)

MARSHALL. All day. Seven days a week. Fifty-two weeks in the year.

KAY. Aye. Between one bottle and another. One bar-room and the next.

FITZPATRICK. Me? I hope you heard all that. I wouldn't touch a drop of liquor.

(MARSHALL *snorts again.*)

I mean, dropping no names, Kay, and all that there and that, aspersions of that nature would be better cast in a different direction altogether.

(FITZPATRICK *gestures at the house.*)

KAY. Some people have a grievance. And some of them haven't.

FITZPATRICK. And what is that supposed to mean?

(KAY *looks at* PAUL, *then looks away.*

The others look at PAUL.)

PAUL. Don't mind me. I'm easy.

KAY. Bennett. Mind that walling.

FITZPATRICK. Are you frightened of telling us something, Kay?

KAY. If you want to work, Fitzpatrick, work. If not, the best thing you can do is to clear off altogether.

(KAY *returns to hang and arrange muslin walling.*)

FITZPATRICK. Ay. Ay, now. Those are very strong words. (*To* MARSHALL) Very strong words indeed.

MARSHALL. If it wasn't for the fact that no trade union would have us ...

FITZPATRICK. I'd repeat that to the man in charge.

MARSHALL. The top official.

FITZPATRICK. Right away.

MARSHALL. Intimidation ...

FITZPATRICK. Suppression of the right to labour.

KAY. You wouldn't know a piece of work, Fitzpatrick, if you saw it. The bloody lot of you ... (*Gestures at the house.*) Poor sod.

(GLENDENNING *has come in, eating a bar of chocolate.*)

FITZPATRICK. Now, then. Now, then. Now, then. What have we got here?

MARSHALL. Come on, now, Glenny. Are you going to let us have a bit of that?

BENNETT. What is it you're eating, Glenny?

GLENDENNING. O ... O ... O ... O ... Oh, A bit of stuff.

FITZPATRICK. A bit of stuff, is it?

GLENDENNING. Ch ... ch ... ch ... ch ... ch ... ch ...

MARSHALL. And have you brought us some of it back?

GLENDENNING. I ... I ... I ... I ... I ... I ...

MARSHALL (*sings*). Ay, yi, yi, yi ... Ay, yi, yi, yi ...

BENNETT. You have, then?

GLENDENNING. Aye!

FITZPATRICK. Chocolate!

(GLENDENNING, *happy, hands out pieces of chocolate, breaking them from the bar.*)

BENNETT. Ah, he's a good lad is Glenny.

FITZPATRICK. I hope he's washed his hands.

(*They laugh.*)

KAY. You better get on with a bit of the walling, Glendenning. (*Looks over at* PAUL.)

MARSHALL. Currying a bit of favour, Kay.

FITZPATRICK. Don't give him any of your sweets, Glenny.

MARSHALL. And don't get too near.

(*They laugh.*

GLENDENNING *starts hanging the muslin wall.*

In the doorway CLAIRE *and* MAURICE *have appeared. They stand on the threshold, looking in. They make some comment to one another and laugh as they watch* PAUL *working, dressing the muslin ropes.*)

MAURICE. Are you enjoying yourself, man?

PAUL. What? (*Looks up.*) I don't know. (*Stands up from the floor where he's been kneeling.*) I've no idea.

MAURICE (*to* CLAIRE). It comes naturally to hand.

CLAIRE (*indicating drapes*). Shouldn't that be a bit higher?

PAUL. Probably. You want to try?

CLAIRE. I was asking.

PAUL. Jolly good.

MAURICE. She's a bloody authority, man.

KAY. Marshall. Over here.

FITZPATRICK. Watch it, Marshy. Watch it.

MARSHALL. Don't worry, now. I shall.

(*They laugh.* KAY *and* MARSHALL *adjust the muslin.*)

FITZPATRICK. And what's it like, then, to be the happy couple? The blushing bride and the handsome groom?

MAURICE. All right, I suppose.

FITZPATRICK. I was never married myself.

(MARSHALL *snorts.*)

I could never find the time.

(MARSHALL *snorts again*.)

MAURICE. No. It is a bit of a problem.

FITZPATRICK (*to* CLAIRE). On the other hand, I could never find a lady, as beautiful as yourself, who'd be glad enough to have me.

BENNETT (*calling*). I'd take no notice of Fitzpatrick. He has a tongue where his brains belong.

FITZPATRICK. I have. It's true. I suffer from over-stimulation. (*To* MAURICE) Have you got a fag?

MAURICE. I have. (*Brings out a case*.)

FITZPATRICK. Now. That makes a pleasant change. (*Takes one*.) I won't smoke it at the present. I'm not allowed. (*Indicates* KAY *with sly gestures*.) But I assure you: I'll enjoy it all the same.

MARSHALL. All the greater, now, for saving it till after.

(FITZPATRICK *laughs and goes back to work*.)

GLENDENNING. Ha ... Ha ... Ha ... Ha ... Ha ... Ha ... Have you seen ... mmmmmmmmmm ... Mister Ewbank?

MAURICE. Wh ... what?

CLAIRE (*to* MAURICE). My dad. (*To* GLENDENNING) No ... We haven't.

GLENDENNING. I ... I ... I ... I ... I ... I ... I ...

MARSHALL (*sings*). Ay, yi, yi, yi ... Ay, yi, yi, yi ...

GLENDENNING. I ... I ... I ... I've got some ... mmmmmmm ... tobacco for him.

CLAIRE. I'll give it to him if you like.

GLENDENNING. I ...I ...I ...

MARSHALL (*sings*). Ay, yi, yi, yi ... Ay, yi, yi, yi ...

GLENDENNING. I ... I ... I'll give it to him.

PAUL. There's not much more now to do.

(OLD EWBANK *has come in with a short piece of rope and wanders round the back of the tent*.)

CLAIRE. I don't know. There's a lot of stuff in the house. He says he wants it bringing out. He's left it a bit late if you ask me.

(PAUL, *having gone back to his work after the last exchange, has got up and crossed over again to* CLAIRE.)

Still. A bit of improvisation might go a long way in here.

PAUL. That's right ...

FITZPATRICK. I heard that. I heard that. A woman who improvises is never to be trusted.

BENNETT (*calling*). And what sort of woman would you trust, Fitzpatrick?

(BENNETT *is polishing the floor where he's kneeling with a rag.*)

FITZPATRICK. Why, Benny, one very much, I think, like you.

(*They all laugh, but for* BENNETT.)

OLD EWBANK. Am I in the way? What? Sitting about in the house.

(*He looks vaguely about him, spots* MARSHALL *and goes over.*)

Here. Now that's a bit of the rope I made.

MARSHALL. Oh. That's ... (*Polishing*)

OLD EWBANK. All by hand. Up and down a rope walk. You wind it up at one end and come up along it with a shuttle. Like this. You can walk up to twenty or thirty miles a day.

MARSHALL. That's a fine bit of rope.

OLD EWBANK. They don't make them like that no more. Machines. A hand-made rope is a bit of the past. (*Gestures up blindly.*) All these: machines.

MARSHALL. Still, they do their job.

(MRS EWBANK *has come in.*)

OLD EWBANK. Good God, man. I've had one all my life. It's my wife who got me to retire. I'd be in here I can tell you if I had a chance.

MRS EWBANK (*to* CLAIRE *and* MAURICE). I've been looking for him all over ... Have you finished in here, Paul?

PAUL. Me personally? Or them in general?

MRS EWBANK. You personally, I think.

PAUL. I'm not sure. I'm standing here, I believe, waiting for instructions.

MRS EWBANK. As long as you're not in the way.

PAUL. I think I've been able to lend a little hand.

MRS EWBANK (*to* CLAIRE). Will he be all right in here?
(*Gesturing at* OLD EWBANK)

MAURICE. He'll be all right. Don't worry.

OLD EWBANK. Good God ... Now what does she want?
(EWBANK *has appeared, oblivious it seems of all of them, carrying two long boxes, five or six feet tall, which will be used to enclose the bottom of the poles. He walks to the centre and puts them down. Over his shoulder are three further lengths of muslin which he'll use to drape the poles, and in his coat pocket is a hammer.*
His mood is one of self-absorption.)

EWBANK. Get out of the bloody way ... God Christ ... Walking all over the bloody floor. God damn and blast. Just look at his bloody boots.

MRS EWBANK (*to* CLAIRE). I'll go in, and make some tea. Keep out of trouble.
(*She goes.*
EWBANK'*s remarks are directed to no one person in particular.*)

OLD EWBANK. Poor? Damn it all, I've never owed a penny to any man!

EWBANK. Put some bloody bags down. Bags. Kay. Get them off here and get it covered. Marshall. Fetch in that other box outside.

(MARSHALL, *after a good look round at* FITZPATRICK, *does so.*

The others begin to cover the floor with the discarded muslin and tent bags.)

OLD EWBANK. When I was sixteen I was working eighteen hours a day.

(FITZPATRICK, *softly, has begun to sing his drinking song.*)

BENNETT. God, look. I've got a splinter in my foot. (*Examines it, sitting on the floor.*)

EWBANK (*to* KAY). If you've got it covered you can't do any harm. Where have I put it? (*Hunts round for his hammer, finding it in his pocket.*) What's he doing in here? (*Seeing* OLD EWBANK)

CLAIRE. He's come to show them his rope.

EWBANK. Rope ... There's a ladder out there, Fitzpatrick.

(MARSHALL *has come in with the third box which he places by the third tent pole.* FITZPATRICK *goes to fetch the ladder.*)

(*Calling after him*) And don't put it down until I tell you.

(*To* KAY) Have these been fastened off? (*Indicating poles*)

KAY. Aye. We've just been doing that.

OLD EWBANK. What's he on about? I'll damn well clip his ear.

MARSHALL (*low to* BENNETT). I wish he bloody would.

EWBANK. What's that? (*Blindly*)

MARSHALL. I say. It's very soft, this wood.

EWBANK. Keep your fingers off it!

(MARSHALL, *working on the floor, draws his hand away.* PAUL, BENNETT, MARSHALL *and* GLENDENNING *are working on the floor.*)

OLD EWBANK. When I was twenty-four I earned thirteen shillings a week.

CLAIRE. Come on, Grandad ... (*Goes to take his arm.*)

OLD EWBANK. I was married when I was nineteen. Three died. Four survived.

(FITZPATRICK *has come in with the ladder.*)

PAUL. Do you want a hand? (*To* CLAIRE)

MAURICE. We'll manage.

(OLD EWBANK, CLAIRE *and* MAURICE *go.*)

FITZPATRICK. Now, then. Where would you want it?

EWBANK. Here, now. Put it down on that ... Gently.

(*He has put a bag at the foot of the first pole and* FITZ-PATRICK *brings the ladder to rest against it.*)

GLENDENNING. I ... I ... I ... I ... I ... I ... I ...

MARSHALL (*sings*). Ay, yi, yi, yi ... Ay, yi, yi, yi ...

(GLENDENNING *has come up to* EWBANK *with the tin of tobacco.*)

EWBANK (*to* FITZPATRICK *as he manoeuvres the ladder*). Gently. Gently. God Christ, do you want to drive it through the floor! Gently!

GLENDENNING. I ... I ... I ... I ...

EWBANK. What? What? What? (*He's busy getting the muslin drapery ready to take up the ladder.*)

BENNETT. He's brought you your tobacco, Mr Ewbank.

EWBANK. What? ... Oh. (*Pauses. Then takes it.*) Aye. You're a good lad.

GLENDENNING. I ... I ... I ... I ...

EWBANK. Did you buy yourself some chocolate?

GLENDENNING. Aye.

(MARSHALL *whistles 'Down Mexico Way' refrain.*)

EWBANK (*to* FITZPATRICK). Hold it. Hold it, Hold it. Hold it. God damn and blast ...

(EWBANK *has turned to the ladder and begun to mount it, hammer in one hand, drapery in the other.*
All the men now, but for GLENDENNING, *and* FITZ-PATRICK, *who is holding the ladder, are working, watching* EWBANK *at the same time.*)

FITZPATRICK (*sings*). Somebody has had a tipple ...

                Somebody has had a drop ...

PAUL. I think we've had enough of that.

FITZPATRICK. What ... ?

PAUL. I think we've had enough of it.

FITZPATRICK. I was just ... (*To* MARSHALL) I have a very melodious voice.

    (BENNETT *snorts*.)

MARSHALL. He has. It's right.

    (FITZPATRICK *shrugs*.

    PAUL *goes back to work*.

    FITZPATRICK, *so the others can see, sings silently, mouthing the words hugely*.)

KAY. All right, Fitzpatrick. You've had your laugh.

EWBANK (*above*). Hold it. God damn and blast.

FITZPATRICK. No hands! (*Stands with his arms out, one foot pressed against the foot of the ladder*.)

KAY. Get that bloody floor rubbed up. Glendenning, do you hear?

GLENDENNING. Aye!

    (FITZPATRICK *looks up to where* EWBANK *is tacking the muslin, draping it round the pole*.)

MARSHALL. Go on. Go on. It'll be over in a flash.

    (*They laugh*.)

EWBANK. I'm coming down ... (*Finishing*)

PAUL (*having crossed over*). Here. I'll hold it.

    (FITZPATRICK *hesitates*.)

    I'll hold it.

    (PAUL *takes the ladder from* FITZPATRICK *who shrugs*.

    EWBANK *comes down the last rungs*.

    Fitzpatrick has gone off, picking up bags, clearing the mess.)

EWBANK (*to* PAUL). If you want summat to do you can

fetch the flowers in from outside. Fitzpatrick, I thought I told you to hold this. Carry it over. (*Indicating the next pole*)

FITZPATRICK (*to* PAUL, *taking it*). Do as the old lad says.

PAUL. I'll hold it. I don't mind. (*To* EWBANK)

EWBANK. Do you think I don't know what goes on. I've got eyes in my backside I have ...

FITZPATRICK. He has. I've seen them.

EWBANK. I miss nowt here. Don't worry. Bennett. Fasten the box round this last pole ...

(PAUL *watches him cross to the next pole where* FITZ-PATRICK *is setting up the ladder. Then he turns and goes.* BENNETT *has begun to fasten the box round the first pole, the end of the muslin, draped round the pole, hung inside. One side of the box is hinged, like a door, and round the top fits a kind of round collar or tray, hinged too so that it can fit round the pole.*)

(*Mounting the ladder and beginning to hang the second drape*) Glendenning, help to bring in those flowers. Marshall ...

MARSHALL. Yes, sir!

EWBANK. When you've got your boots off start at that end polishing the floor.

FITZPATRICK. Good God. It's come at last.

MARSHALL. My boots?

FITZPATRICK. He can't mean it.

EWBANK. Get on with it. Get on ... (*To* FITZPATRICK) Hold that ladder!

(MARSHALL *takes off his boots and begins, at the farthest end, with a mop and duster, to polish the floor.*)

Thousands on his education ... Bloody flowers. Six bob an hour.

(KAY *is finishing off the floor and then adjusts the drapes round the walls.*

PAUL *has begun to carry in the flowers, arranging them round the box that* BENNETT *has fastened.*)

FITZPATRICK (*to* EWBANK). Can you see up there all right?

EWBANK. I can see, all right. Don't worry.

FITZPATRICK. Which pair, now, is it that you're using?

(MARSHALL, BENNETT *and* FITZPATRICK *laugh.*)

EWBANK. Hold it, now. I'm coming down ... Bennett. Let's have the other box round here. God damn and blast, I can see somebody's feet marks from up here. Kay, just watch it ... Boots. Boots. Boots, man. Boots. (*As he reaches the ground*) Here, Fitzpatrick. You take it. Hammer. Tacks. Drape. Have it up on that last pole.

FITZPATRICK. Me?

(MARSHALL *has begun to laugh, giggling.*)

EWBANK. I'm not talking to the bloody floor?

FITZPATRICK. No ...

EWBANK. Right, then. Get on with it. (*To* KAY) I'm not so bloody silly as I look.

MARSHALL. No, no. He's probably right, at that.

EWBANK. What's that?

MARSHALL (*indicating floor where he's polishing*). I say, there's a hell of a shine, on that.

EWBANK (*to* KAY). You'll find the tables out there. The chairs as well.

KAY (*going*). Glendenning. Here, give me a hand.

EWBANK (*looking up at the interior*). I shall never do it again. I shan't. Never ...

(BENNETT *is fastening the box and its collar round the second pole.*

FITZPATRICK *has carried the ladder over to the third pole and begun to climb it, tacking up the drape.*

OLD MRS EWBANK *comes in carrying a pot plant with a splendid flower.*

75

PAUL *is arranging the flowers now round the second pole as*
BENNETT *finishes the box.*

MARSHALL *polishes the floor, starting the farthest end and
now working towards the middle, leaving it clear behind him.
The whole interior now has slowly fallen into shape, a gentle
radiance coming through the drapes.*

KAY *and* GLENDENNING *have begun to bring in the rest
of the white, wrought-iron tables: they're small and neat,
with chairs to match. They set them round the edge of the
floor.)*

OLD MRS E. Where shall I put it?

FITZPATRICK (*calling down*). The lady here ... wants to know
where you'd like her to put it.

PAUL. Here. I'll take it.

OLD MRS E. (*admiring the flowers*). It's very nice.

PAUL. Yes. Just about.

OLD MRS E. He has a great flair with flowers.

EWBANK. What?

OLD MRS E. Paul.

EWBANK. Aye. (*To* BENNETT) I'll finish that. You can get
out now and start loading the truck.

MARSHALL (*calling*). He's going to put his boots on.

FITZPATRICK (*calling*). What?

MARSHALL. He's going to put his boots on.

FITZPATRICK. Thank God for that. (*Wafts his nose.*) The
atmosphere up here is damn near revolting.

EWBANK. Marshall, finish off that floor. I want you out of
here now, as quick as you can.

MARSHALL. It'll be over in a jiffy ... (*Polishing*)

(EWBANK *himself has taken the box over to the last post.*)

EWBANK. Come on. Come on, Fitzpatrick. I could have
fastened up half a dozen.

FITZPATRICK. I'm coming. I'm coming. Now clear the
decks.

MARSHALL. Steady as she goes.

FITZPATRICK. Steady as she goes. You're right.
(*He comes down, and starts to take the ladder out.*
EWBANK *begins to fasten on the box.*)

OLD MRS E. (*to* PAUL). I'll give you a hand. If you like. (*She helps to arrange the flowers.*) Was your Grandad in here?

PAUL. With his bit of rope.

EWBANK. He'll bloody hang himself with it one of these days. (*To the* MEN) Come on. Come on.
(OLD MRS EWBANK *gestures in the direction of* EWBANK *and* PAUL *nods his head.*)

OLD MRS E. There are some more in the house to come across I think.

PAUL (*still arranging*). It's all right. I'll fetch them. There's no hurry.

OLD MRS E. No, no. I'd like to help ... (*She goes out.*)
(FITZPATRICK *has come back after taking out the ladder. He begins to take out odds and ends, setting chairs, winking at* MARSHALL *who is still polishing, making him laugh.*)

EWBANK (*to* KAY). You've fastened off them guys, I take it.
(*Indicating outside*)

KAY. Aye. Aye. They're all right. We're nearly ready for off.

EWBANK. You've got to watch every damn thing yourself in this place, Kay. If you don't, not one ... not one do you ever get done ... Who the hell's that shouting? (*To* FITZPATRICK) Get out of here, now. Go on. Clear off.
(KAY *collects bags from floor and goes.*)

FITZPATRICK. Have we finished?

EWBANK. Finished? You were finished long ago. You want to think yourself damn lucky there's somebody here'll employ you.

FITZPATRICK. Oh, I do. I do. Those are lovely flowers.

EWBANK. Get out. Go on. Clear off. Marshall, you clear off
with him.

MARSHALL. Thank the Lord for that. (*Going*) It's been a hard
day, now. It has.

> (*The whole place now has been cleared: the floor shining, the
> men crossing it on tip-toe. The white tables and chairs have
> been set round the sides, bowls of flowers put on them, PAUL
> completing this and arranging flowers round the last of the
> three poles as EWBANK finishes fastening the box.*
>
> *Gradually the whole place is cleared, leaving, finally,
> EWBANK and PAUL alone.*)

EWBANK. I said arrange them, lad. Not plant them.

PAUL. That's all right. Don't worry. None of these'll
grow.

EWBANK (*looking up at awning*). It's not straight even now ...
I don't know. All that damn care and trouble.

PAUL. Don't worry.

EWBANK. What ... ?

> (EWBANK *is suddenly aware that he and* PAUL *are alone.*)

Aye. Well ...

> (*They both fall silent.*
>
> *For some little while* PAUL *works quietly at the flowers,*
> EWBANK *standing in the centre of the tent, still.*
>
> KAY *suddenly comes in.*)

KAY. I've checked on all the guys. Slacked them off for the
night ...

> (*He glances at them both, he himself still standing in the
> door.*)

The truck's loaded ... I'll get them back down, then. To
the yard.

EWBANK. Aye.

KAY. Well, then. I'll say good night.

EWBANK. That's right.

PAUL. See you.

KAY. Aye. Right, then ...

> (KAY *nods and goes.*
> *Silence. Then:*)

EWBANK. Do you ever fancy this job?

> (PAUL *looks up.*
>
> EWBANK *gestures at the tent.*)

This.

> (PAUL *looks round. Then, after a moment, he shakes his head.*)

Aye. Well ... I'm not surprised. (*Briskly*) Not much thanks you get for it.

PAUL. No.

EWBANK. Aye. Well ... (*Pause. Then:*)

> (FITZPATRICK *pops his head in.* MARSHALL *is just behind him.*)

FITZPATRICK. I'll say good night then. Looks a picture.

MARSHALL. Wouldn't mind living here meself.

FITZPATRICK. You should see his bloody room.

MARSHAL. An hovel.

FITZPATRICK. Pig-sty.

MARSHALL. It is. He's right.

BENNETT (*popping in behind*). We'll say good night, then, er ... er.

EWBANK. Aye. Right-o.

FITZPATRICK. Right, then. Let's be off.

MARSHALL. Good luck tomorrow.

EWBANK. Aye.

FITZPATRICK (*going*). They'll need it, now, all right.

> (*They go.*)

MARSHALL (*off*). Come on, now, Glenny ...

GLENDENNING (*off*). Aye!

> (GLENDENNING *appears in doorway.*)

G ... g ... g ... g ... g ... g ...

79

EWBANK. Aye. Good night, lad. I'll see you at the yard tomorrow.

GLENDENNING. I ... I ... I ... I ... I ... I ...

MARSHALL (*sings off*). Ay, yi, yi, yi ... Ay, yi, yi, yi.

EWBANK. Aye. Thanks for the tobacco.

GLENDENNING. Mmmmmmmmmmmm ... (*Can't get it out.*)

PAUL. Bye, Glenny.

(PAUL *gets up now from the flowers.*)

GLENDENNING. See you ... mmmmmm ... d-day after to-morrow!

PAUL. Aye. That's right.

GLENDENNING (*gesturing at tent*). I ... I ... I ... I ... I ...

MARSHALL (*sings off*). Ay, yi, yi, yi ... Ay, yi, yi, yi ...

GLENDENNING. Lovely.

PAUL. Aye ...

GLENDENNING. W ... w ... w ... well ... (*Nods and grins at them.*)

FITZPATRICK (*off*). Come on, Glenny. We're going to be here all night.

MARSHALL (*off*). Spends forty-eight hours, does Glenny, saying good morning.

EWBANK. Get off, lad. Or they'll be gone without you.

GLENDENNING. Aye!

(*He smiles at them, then goes.*

EWBANK *and* PAUL *stand silently in the tent. Vaguely they look around.*)

EWBANK. You know. You mustn't mind them ... (*Gestures off.*)

PAUL. Oh ... (*Realizing*) No.

EWBANK. They've a mind for nowt, you know.

PAUL. Yes ... (*Nods.*)

EWBANK. It'll not happen again, you know ...

(PAUL *looks up at him.*

EWBANK *gestures round.*)
This.

PAUL. There'll not be the chance.

EWBANK. Too bloody old to start again.

PAUL. Aye.

EWBANK. Ah ... well, then ...
    (*Pause.*)

PAUL. Aye ... Well ... I'll go and fetch some flowers.
    (PAUL *goes.*
    EWBANK *stands gazing at the tent.*
    He leans up after a moment against one of the boxes, his arm
    stretched to it, contemplative.
    OLD MRS EWBANK *comes in quietly, unnoticed, carrying*
    a plant. She puts it in place, regards it.
    Then, seeing EWBANK, *she looks up.*)

OLD MRS E. Oh ... It's lovely.

EWBANK. Aye.
    (MRS EWBANK *has come in, admiring.*)
    (MRS EWBANK *enters.*)

OLD MRS E. It's finished, love. D'you like it?

MRS EWBANK (*nods, coming farther in*). Well, then ... They
    should be pleased. (*To* EWBANK)

EWBANK. Aye.

OLD MRS E. I'll ... There are one or two more to fetch in.
    (EWBANK *nods.*)
    OLD MRS EWBANK *goes.*)

MRS EWBANK. Have the men gone?

EWBANK. That's right.
    (MRS EWBANK *comes farther in, looking round.*)

MRS EWBANK. Is it what you were hoping for?

EWBANK. Hoping?

MRS EWBANK (*pause*). He's done the flowers well ...

EWBANK (*looking up at the tent*). Come today. Gone to-
    morrow.

MRS EWBANK (*watches him. Then:*) Ah, well.

EWBANK. Aye ...

> (CLAIRE *and* MAURICE *appear at the door after a moment, looking in together.*)

MAURICE. Can we come in? Is it all right to enter?

EWBANK. Aye. That's what it's for.

MRS EWBANK. Come in ...

CLAIRE. It's lovely. (*Slides across the floor in a vague dance.*) Super. (*To* MAURICE) What do you think?

MAURICE (*standing in the centre, gazing up*). Lovely.

MRS EWBANK (*to both*). Well ... I'm glad you like it.

CLAIRE. Course we do. Why not?

MRS EWBANK. Tell your dad. Not me.

CLAIRE. 'Thanks, old man,' she said.

EWBANK. Aye.

MAURICE. Lovely.

> (PAUL *has come in quietly at the back with flowers.*
> OLD EWBANK *comes in carrying a piece of rope, entering quite confidently, only then, as he reaches the centre, looking round, aware that it isn't as it was before.*
> OLD MRS EWBANK *has come in after him.*)

OLD EWBANK. Where are they? I've brought him another bit to look at.

MRS EWBANK. They've gone.

PAUL. On the lorry.

OLD EWBANK. I damn well would. It's not often you get the chance.

MAURICE. Wanna dance?

CLAIRE. Sure. (*Holds out her hands.*)

MRS EWBANK. Do you think you should ...

CLAIRE. Why not? (*Laughing*)

MRS EWBANK. I don't know ... (*Laughs.*) I'm not sure.

MAURICE. 'S bad luck.

CLAIRE. Luck never came into it.

(*She laughs and dances tentatively with* MAURICE *round the floor.*)

CLAIRE. Aren't you going to give your mother a dance, Paul?

PAUL. I don't know ... If she wants one.

(MRS EWBANK *shrugs, pleased.*)

MRS EWBANK. I don't mind. If you think you can manage ...
(*She laughs.*)

PAUL. Mind me hands. Black. (*Holds them up.*)

(*He holds her tentatively, and they dance round with some pleasure.*)

OLD EWBANK. I've never seen ought like it. Can you turn up the sound?

OLD MRS E. (*crossing to him*). There isn't any. Here ... Sit down.
(*They sit at one of the tables.*)

MAURICE. Ought to break out a few drinks. What? Celebrate.

MRS EWBANK. Oh, there's plenty enough time for that.

CLAIRE. In any case. We're not hitched.

MAURICE. Not yet.

MRS EWBANK. Oh, now. Don't let's start on that.

CLAIRE (*gestures at tent*). If only for this we have no option.
(*They laugh.*)

PAUL. Do you want to dance with my mother, Dad?

EWBANK. Aye. I'll give her a dance. Why not?

(EWBANK *takes* MRS EWBANK *firmly.*

They begin to dance, whirling round in an old-fashioned waltz.

MAURICE *and* CLAIRE *have stopped dancing to watch.*

EWBANK *and* MRS EWBANK *dance round the whole tent.*

EWBANK'S *dancing is heavy, firm and implacable, entirely characteristic of himself.*)

MRS EWBANK. Wow! Wow! Not so fast.

MAURICE. I'd say ... He was a drop or two ahead of us.

CLAIRE (*puts her finger to her lips, shaking her head*). Aye, now. That's enough.

MAURICE. Go on, Dad. Let 'em have it.

(EWBANK *and* MRS EWBANK *dance on.*)

EWBANK (*stopping*). Theer now.

MRS EWBANK. Oh. Goodness. (*Holds her head, pulls back her hair.*) Am I still in one piece? (*To* CLAIRE. *She staggers, laughing.*) Oh, dear. I'm spinning.

OLD EWBANK. If I had my time o'er again, I'd burn the bloody lot.

PAUL. What's that?

OLD EWBANK. Machines. It's never too late. Bloody burn them, and that's that.

CLAIRE. If he's like this now, what's he going to be like tomorrow?

OLD EWBANK (*holding rope*). A bit of pressure, and they come to pieces in your hand.

OLD MRS E. I'll take him in and let him lie down.

EWBANK. Aye ... He needs looking after.

OLD EWBANK. I worked thirty or forty hours a day.

OLD MRS E. He means at week-ends.

OLD EWBANK (*going*). What? If I'd had any more I'd have given him a bit ...

OLD MRS E. Oh, well. We might find a piece or two you've forgotten.

OLD EWBANK. By God. They are. One glance and they damn well come apart.

(*They go.*

EWBANK *sits.*

Silence.)

MRS EWBANK. Well, then ...

(*Pause. Then:*)

PAUL. I'll go in and wash up. (*Looking at his hands*)

MAURICE. Yes. Well, I better be getting home ...

CLAIRE. I'll get your things.

MAURICE (*to* MRS EWBANK). I'll see you later. This evening.

MRS EWBANK. Yes. Later on.

(*They go.*)

CLAIRE. And tonight, try and stay ...

MAURICE. What?

CLAIRE. Sober.

(EWBANK *and* MRS EWBANK *are left alone.*

They are silent. Then:)

MRS EWBANK. Well. All ready.

EWBANK. Aye.

(*They are silent. Then:*)

MRS EWBANK. Are you coming in?

(EWBANK *looks up.*)

Spend your last evening with your daughter.

EWBANK. Aye ... (*He looks up at the finished tent.*)

MRS EWBANK. We'll manage.

EWBANK. Aye. We'll make a damn good job of it. (*Half-laughs.*) ... We will.

MRS EWBANK. Well, then. (*Going*) Aren't you coming?
(*Goes.*)

(EWBANK *gazes round, picks up the old piece of rope* OLD
EWBANK *has left. Gazes round. Rises. Goes.*
(*Slowly the light fades.*)

END OF ACT TWO

ACT THREE

Early morning.

The tent has suffered a great deal. Part of the muslin drapery hangs loosely down. Similarly, parts of the lining round the walls hang down in loose folds, unhooked, or on the floor. Part of the dance floor itself has been removed, other parts uprooted and left in loose slabs: chairs have been upturned, tables left lying on their sides. Bottles lie here and there on the floor, along with discarded napkins, streamers, tablecloths, paper-wrapping. Most of the flowers have gone and the few that remain have been dragged out of position, ready to be disposed of.

GLENDENNING (*heard*). I ... I ... I ... I ... I ...

MARSHALL (*heard, sings*). Ay, yi, yi, yi ... Ay, yi, yi, yi.

FITZPATRICK (*heard*). Wakey-wakey!

BENNETT (*heard*). Not a word ...

> (FITZPATRICK *trips and falls into the door, regaining his balance as he stumbles into the tent.*)

FITZPATRICK. Good grief and God help us ... Et cetera and all that ...

> (BENNETT *has come in behind him after a few moments. He too stands dazed, looking round.*)

GLENDENNING (*heard*). I ... I ... I ... I ...

MARSHALL (*heard, sings*). Ay, yi, yi, yi ... Ay, yi, yi, yi.

FITZPATRICK. Somebody's been enjoying themselves. I'd say, at a very quick guess ... (*Picks up a bottle, examines it, finds it empty, puts it down.*) At a very quick guess indeed, I'd say there was nothing left.

BENNETT. There's not a lot left here for us to do, Fitzie ...

FITZPATRICK. There's not. There's not ... Just look at that.
(*Indicates some damage.*)

    (KAY *has come in the other side, lifting the walling and
stooping underneath.*)

(*Calling off*) Come in here, Marshy, old man. This should
impress you all right.

KAY. Mind the floor ... Don't step on any glass.

MARSHALL (*appearing*). Good God. And may the saints
preserve us.

FITZPATRICK. More empty bottles, Marshy, than even you
can count.

MARSHALL. And me not a drinking man, either.

FITZPATRICK (*laughs*). No. No. And you not a drinking man
at all.

MARSHALL. That's a rare old sight indeed. (*Picks up a bottle.*)

FITZPATRICK. And not a drop to have.

MARSHALL. I wouldn't at all, now, like to be the one to foot
the bill.

    (*He puts the bottle down and, like* FITZPATRICK, *drifts
around the interior inspecting the bottles.*

    GLENDENNING *has come in, eating a sandwich.*)

GLENDENNING. Th ... th ... th ... th ... that's a good old ...
mmmmm ... mmmmess.

KAY. You better start on the bottles, Fitzpatrick.

    (MARSHALL *roars with laughter.*)

FITZPATRICK. And what's so funny about that?

MARSHALL (*to* KAY). Ah, now, if they'd sent him down to
yonder ... (*Thumbs down.*) That'd be just the job they'd
find.

FITZPATRICK (*picking up bottles*). Empty ... empty ... every
one.

KAY. Marshall. You help him. And with the mess as well.

    (FITZPATRICK *roars with laughter.*)

Bennett ... (*Indicates tables.*) Glendenning ... (*Indicates chairs.*)

GLENDENNING. I ... I ... I ... Aye!

MARSHALL. Don't you ever get tired of eatin', Glenny?

FITZPATRICK (*holding bottle to light*). And where now, do you think, is the happy bride?

(*He drinks off the dregs, grimaces, holds his stomach.*)

BENNETT. Not here, for one. That's sure.

MARSHALL. I don't know. Might find half a dozen under the table, if this place is any indication to go by at all.

BENNETT. God. God. But it's freezing.

MARSHALL (*holding bottle up, gazing at it*). Ice.

GLENDENNING. I ... I ... I ... I ...

MARSHALL (*sings*). Ay, yi, yi, yi ... Ay, yi, yi, yi ...

GLENDENNING. I ... I ... I ... I ... Ice!

FITZPATRICK. In summer, Glenny.

BENNETT. It's damn near autumn now.

MARSHALL. What?

GLENDENNING. Aye!

MARSHALL (*drinking dregs*). To God! It's glass! (*Spits out.*)

(FITZPATRICK *laughs.*

GLENDENNING *and* BENNETT *laugh.*)

FITZPATRICK. You mad Patrick. You'll never learn.

MARSHALL. It's glass. God damn it! I've nearly cut meself to death!

FITZPATRICK. A bloody booby-trap. (*Doubles up with laughter at* MARSHALL'*s discomposure.*) Watch out!

KAY. I said take it outside.

BENNETT. That stuff'll poison you.

KAY. Glendenning, *chairs.*

GLENDENNING (*happy*). Aye!

FITZPATRICK. And what, now, do you think of that?

BENNETT. What is it?

FITZPATRICK. A lady's undergarment, or I'm a frog.

    (*Holds up a piece of muslin.*)

KAY. It is not. (*Looks up at lining.*)

BENNETT. It's off the lining. Some madman has torn it down.

MARSHALL. He'll go through the tent top. When he sees all this.

FITZPATRICK. God damn and blast.

KAY. What is it?

    (FITZPATRICK *looks frantically about him.*)

FITZPATRICK. Me hammer. Me hammer ... I've lost it. (*To* GLENDENNING) God damn it. Will you go find it in the cab?

GLENDENNING. Aye!

    (GLENDENNING *immediately puts down the chair he's carrying, nods, and goes quickly outside.*)

BENNETT. You want to leave him alone ...

MARSHALL. What?

BENNETT. Glendenning.

MARSHALL. Ah, now. Go jump on your bloody head.

BENNETT (*backs down*). God. It's freezing. (*Shivers.*)

    (*They continue working.* KAY *has begun to take down the muslin walls.*)

KAY. Marshall, will you bring in the muslin bags.

MARSHALL. Aye. Aye. (*To* BENNETT) It's me today. Fitzpatrick, no doubt it'll be you tomorrow.

FITZPATRICK (*looking round again*). Good God, you know, but this is a bloody mess.

BENNETT. Aye. Aye ...

    (MARSHALL *comes back in with the bags.*)

FITZPATRICK (*to* KAY). Have you seen Ewbank this morning?

KAY. I have not. (*Still working*)

MARSHALL. Steady. Steady. Might find him underneath all that. (*Indicates floor.*)

FITZPATRICK. No. No. Up! He's not there at all.

(GLENDENNING *has come back in.*)

KAY. You better keep your boots off just the same.
Marshall ...

(*Indicates* MARSHALL *to help him with the muslin walling:
wrap it and put it in the bags.*

BENNETT *has started sweeping the paper streamers and
debris off the floor.*

GLENDENNING *has resumed work as though nothing has
happened, picking up the chairs, carrying them out, ex-
pressionless, not looking up.*)

MARSHALL. Ay, now. And where's that hammer? Here's
Fitzpatrick waiting to have a smash.

FITZPATRICK. I am. I am. That's right.

BENNETT. You want to leave him alone, Fitzpatrick.

MARSHALL (*innocent*). Was I intending any harm? (*Indicating*
GLENDENNING) He wouldn't know what to do with-
out us.

FITZPATRICK. Have you noticed how — of recent times, I'm
speaking — Bennett has grown quite dictatorial in his
habits? (*Starts taking up the floor.*)

MARSHALL. He has.

FITZPATRICK. Censorious, if I didn't know him better.

MARSHALL. Censorious is the word.

FITZPATRICK. And we all know, now, the reason for it.

MARSHALL. Reason? Is there a reason, too, for that? (*Gazing
up.*)

FITZPATRICK. It's explained, Benny, is it not, easily enough?

(BENNETT *goes on working.* KAY *looks up briefly then
continues.*)

MARSHALL. Now, now. You'll have to tell us all the
rest.

FITZPATRICK. Benny here is the one you ought to ask.

(BENNETT *glances up at* FITZPATRICK, *then continues with his work.*

GLENDENNING *comes and goes with the remaining chairs and tables and the odd bits of rubbish.*)

MARSHALL. No, no. We're going to get nothing out of that.

KAY. Fitzpatrick ... (*Indicates he get on with his work.*)

(FITZPATRICK *gets on, clearing the rest of the rubbish, bottles, etc. then starting on the floor.*)

FITZPATRICK. It's quite easy to explain, nevertheless, and though I might well be wrong in detail, the whole mass, as it were, is treasonably correct.

MARSHALL. Go on. Go on, I'm listening. Kay, have you opened up an ear? Would you mind, Glenny, now, if you left the room?

GLENDENNING. Aye!

FITZPATRICK. His wife left him for another man.

MARSHALL. She did!

FITZPATRICK. She did.

MARSHALL. As long as it wasn't for another woman.

(MARSHALL *and* FITZPATRICK *laugh.*)

To God. And whoever would have thought of that? A man with a face like that ...

FITZPATRICK. And figure.

MARSHALL. And figure.

FITZPATRICK. And boots.

MARSHALL. And boots.

FITZPATRICK. Socks.

MARSHALL. Socks.

FITZPATRICK. Teeth. (*Showing his*)

MARSHALL. Teeth. (*Showing his*)

FITZPATRICK. Smiling ... (*Smiles.*)

MARSHALL. Smiling ...

BENNETT. Your mouth's going to open too wide one of these days, Fitzpatrick.

FITZPATRICK. It'll be all the easier to let the truth come flying out.

BENNETT. And for me to put my fist inside it.

FITZPATRICK. Since when has a man like me let a man like you put his fist inside my mouth?

(MARSHALL *laughs.*

BENNETT *tenses but doesn't answer.*)

KAY. Fitzpatrick, get out, and load the truck outside.

FITZPATRICK. On my own? God damn it. I'm only human.

MARSHALL. Almost.

FITZPATRICK. Almost. (*Going*) It's a hard bloody life is this: walk the straight and narrow and you end up working by yourself. (*He goes.*)

MARSHALL. Well. Well. Now there's a thing. (*Tuts away to himself.*) Revelations.

BENNETT. And it's not only Fitzpatrick.

MARSHALL. Not only what?

BENNETT. Who'll feel the end of this. (*Holds up his fist.*)

MARSHALL. What? What? ... You're not thinking ... You can't mean it?

(BENNETT *gazes steadily at him, obviously unable to carry out his threat, then turns and goes back to his work.*)

Good God. He can.

(FITZPATRICK *can be heard singing outside.*

Silence for a moment inside the tent.)

Do you think now ...

(BENNETT *looks up threateningly.*)

(*Spreading his arms*) We'd get anything back on the bottles.

(*They go back to work.*

FITZPATRICK *pops his head in.*)

FITZPATRICK. I can hear Mr Ewbank singing.

KAY. Singing ... ?

FITZPATRICK. Round the back side of the house ... (*Pops out.*)

MARSHALL. There's a blue sky around the corner.

FITZPATRICK (*listens*). Beautiful.

MARSHALL. Like a bird ...

FITZPATRICK. Like a bird.

KAY. Fitzpatrick ...

FITZPATRICK (*indicating house*). Must be in a great good humour.

MARSHALL. Great good humour: I think you're right.

FITZPATRICK. Tucked up warm and cosy.

MARSHALL. Warm and cosy.

FITZPATRICK. Shaving.

MARSHALL. Mirror ...

FITZPATRICK. Hot water.

MARSHALL. Fingers ...

FITZPATRICK. Toes.

KAY. Fitzpatrick!

FITZPATRICK. All right. All right.

> (FITZPATRICK *goes.*
> BENNETT *has started taking up the floor;* GLENDENNING *takes the pieces out.*
> KAY *is detaching the muslin roof from the walls, letting it fall to the centre of the tent, where it hangs like a sail.*
> MARSHALL *himself now has started on the floor.*)

MARSHALL. How many hours, now, Glenny, do you sleep at night?

GLENDENNING. Aye!

MARSHALL. And how many hours is that? (*To* KAY) I don't think Glenny sleeps at all. Like a damn great owl, sitting there, his eyes wide open.

94

GLENDENNING. Aye! (*He watches them, pleased, then takes out floor.*)

BENNETT. I never need more than six or seven.

MARSHALL. Six or seven ... ?

BENNETT. Hours.

MARSHALL. Hours ... I thought ... Ah, well. But then ...

BENNETT. What's that? (*Genially*)

MARSHALL. A separated man ... You can never sleep long, on your own, in a single bed.

(BENNETT *seems about to turn on him.*)

(*To* KAY) It's true, then, Kay. They put a man like you inside.

FITZPATRICK (*popping back*). There's many a better man been put in with him.

MARSHALL. There has. There has ... Still singing?

FITZPATRICK (*shakes head, picks up piece of flooring*). Having, I think, a little rest.

MARSHALL. Recuperation. No sound of breathing? No shouts? No cries.

FITZPATRICK. Not a bird. Not a twitter.

MARSHALL. Resting then. No doubt. A damn great house like that ...

FITZPATRICK. He's worked hard now, Marshy, for every penny he's got.

MARSHALL. He has. You're right. And we as well, now, have worked a damn sight harder.

(FITZPATRICK *laughs, taking up more of the dance floor.*)

MARSHALL. It looks to me like a damn great orgy ...

KAY. What's that?

FITZPATRICK. He pricked his ears at that.

MARSHALL. I shouldn't wonder. Just look at that. Scratches ...

BENNETT. That's made with glass.

MARSHALL. Glass? I'd have sworn it was somebody's fingers ... Dragged out. Protesting to the last.

(They laugh. BENNETT *and* GLENDENNING *carry out pieces. Then:)*

If you ask me, they're both heading hard for trouble.

FITZPATRICK. Who?

MARSHALL. The bridegroom and the bride.

(They're both taking up the floor, waiting for BENNETT *to return.)*

FITZPATRICK. Oh, now. What makes you feel like that?

MARSHALL *(as* BENNETT *returns).* Experience, man. Marriage, as an institution—in my opinion—is all washed out. Finished ... Kaput.

FITZPATRICK *(towards* BENNETT*).* Ah, now. There speaks a knowledgeable man.

MARSHALL. I do. I am.

KAY. All right, now. Let's have it down.

*(*KAY *has now released the muslin roof from the sides of the tent and it hangs in a single drape down the centre of the tent.* FITZPATRICK *goes on clearing the floor; the others go to the ropes to lower the muslin.)*

FITZPATRICK. Bus-conductor ...

MARSHALL. Rose nearly to inspector, but for her sex, Fitzpatrick.

FITZPATRICK. But for our sex, Marshy, and we'd all rise to something else, Greengrocer's right-hand assistant. Nun ...

MARSHALL. Baked apple-pie. *(Lowering)*

FITZPATRICK. Is that a fact?

MARSHALL. So many apples in, they nearly tore the crust apart.

FITZPATRICK. Good God. Glenny! I hope you're listening.

GLENDENNING. Aye!

FITZPATRICK. I wonder if old Benny's was a cook?

(He goes, carrying the floor.
The muslin now is lowered. BENNETT *looks up wildly,*

96

then he goes on with the others untaping the muslin from the ridges and unlacing it at the seams.)

MARSHALL *(untaping).* I knew a man once. Came home from work one afternoon ... Been let off early – an act of charity – by the boss ...

BENNETT. Aye?

MARSHALL. Found his wife in bed with another man.

(BENNETT *looks across.*)

KAY. Be careful where you let it fall.

MARSHALL. Comes in. Finds no dinner. Goes upstairs. Commotion ... Opens door ...

FITZPATRICK *(returning).* And Bob's your uncle.

MARSHALL. No. No. You weren't the one I had in mind at all.

(*They laugh.*)

KAY *(to* FITZPATRICK). Side poles ...

FITZPATRICK. Good God ... I was getting used, now, to trotting off outside.

MARSHALL. Aren't you going to let me finish my story?

FITZPATRICK. Hung up a notice.

MARSHALL. What?

FITZPATRICK. Hung up a notice: DO NOT DISTURB, outside.

(FITZPATRICK *and* MARSHALL *laugh.*)

KAY. All right, now. All right. Let's have it in the bags.

(*The men start to pack the three separated pieces of muslin lining.*

FITZPATRICK *has started to remove the side poles.*)

MARSHALL. I've been badly suited, I have, in the matter of fidelity.

FITZPATRICK. Easy come ...

MARSHALL. That's what they say.

KAY. Careful ... gently.

(MARSHALL *and* FITZPATRICK *laugh*.)

BENNETT. I've told you, Fitzpatrick. That's the last chance
you'll have.

FITZPATRICK. That's what I said ...

MARSHALL. She didn't believe me.

(MARSHALL *and* FITZPATRICK *laugh*.)

GLENDENNING. I ... I ... I ... I ... I ...

MARSHALL (*sings*). Ay, yi, yi, yi ... Ay, yi, yi, yi ...

(GLENDENNING *takes out the bagged muslin.*
BENNETT *is now releasing the ropes from the muslin
ridges.*)

FITZPATRICK. A faithful wife ...

MARSHALL. Is like a stone round your neck ...

FITZPATRICK. No decent man would be seen without it.

(FITZPATRICK *and* MARSHALL *laugh*.)

KAY. Fitzpatrick. Shut your mouth.

FITZPATRICK. It's Bennett ...

BENNETT. You've had your chance, Fitzpatrick.

MARSHALL. You've had your chance, Fitzpatrick.

FITZPATRICK. That's what she said.

(MARSHALL *and* FITZPATRICK *laugh*.)

KAY (*to* MARSHALL). If you call that work, you better get
yourself another job.

MARSHALL (*horrified*). Another!

FITZPATRICK. God. That's the worst thing I've ever
heard.

(MARSHALL *shakes his head, clearing out either ear with
his little finger.*)

KAY. Marshall ... Fitzpatrick ... (*Indicates the floor.*) Bennett ...
(*The men start taking up the rest of the floor.*)

MARSHALL. Trade unions.

FITZPATRICK. What?

MARSHALL. Trade unions.

(BENNETT *looks up, then continues taking out the floor*

98

with GLENDENNING *as* MARSHALL *and* FITZPATRICK
lift it.)

FITZPATRICK. That's an interesting proposition.

MARSHALL. It is.

FITZPATRICK. Why certain people ...

MARSHALL. Who shall be nameless ...

FITZPATRICK. Come seeking employment ...

MARSHALL. Of all places ...

FITZPATRICK. At Mr Ewbank's place itself.

MARSHALL. Aye.

FITZPATRICK. Tenting contractor ...

MARSHALL. For all outside ...

FITZPATRICK. And inside occasions.

(*They laugh.*)

(*Direct to* MARSHALL) Some of course ...

MARSHALL. Have no alternative ... No. No. They haven't.
That's right.

FITZPATRICK. In a manner of speaking, they have no choice.

MARSHALL. No, no. That's right. They can't be blamed.

FITZPATRICK. While on the other hand ...

MARSHALL. You're right. You're right.

FITZPATRICK. Some of them ...

MARSHALL. You're right.

FITZPATRICK. Come here because they're bone idle.

MARSHALL. Like myself you mean.

FITZPATRICK. Like yourself. On the other hand ...

MARSHALL. Aye ...

FITZPATRICK. There are those ...

MARSHALL. Aye ...

FITZPATRICK. Who have it in them to rise to higher things.

MARSHALL. Higher things. They have.

FITZPATRICK. Who have, within them, Marshy, the capacity
to get on.

MARSHALL. They have. They have. You're right.

FITZPATRICK. But who, suddenly—through some calamity on the domestic front ...

MARSHALL. The domestic front ...

FITZPATRICK. In a manner of speaking ...

MARSHALL. In a manner of speaking. That's right.

FITZPATRICK. Lose ...

MARSHALL. Lose.

FITZPATRICK. All interest in carrying on.

MARSHALL. They do. They do. You're right.

FITZPATRICK. Some terrible calamity overwhelms them ...

MARSHALL. ... on the domestic front ...

FITZPATRICK. And up, into the wide blue yonder ... all pride and initiative: gone.

MARSHALL. Aye ... Vanished.

BENNETT. I'm not above using this, Fitzpatrick!

(BENNETT *has come in and has wrapped one of the muslin ropes: now he threatens* FITZPATRICK *with the shackle end.*)

FITZPATRICK. No, no. Each man to his tools I've always said.

MARSHALL (*to* FITZPATRICK). A tradesman from his tools should never be divided.

BENNETT. I'll kill you. I bloody will!

KAY. That's enough, Fitzpatrick.

FITZPATRICK. I was merely ascertainin' the truth of the matter, Kay.

MARSHALL (*to* FITZPATRICK). What's a man's life worth if it's comprised of nothing but untruths and lies?

FITZPATRICK. What is it now, indeed?

KAY. And what's so remarkable about your life, Fitzpatrick?

FITZPATRICK. Remarkable?

KAY. That it gives you the right to go poking so often into other people's.

(GLENDENNING *has come in slowly.*)

A loud-mouth. A wet rag. That doesn't do a crumb of work unless he's driven to it.

(KAY *has crossed slowly over to* FITZPATRICK.)

FITZPATRICK. Loud-mouth, now, I might be. And bone-idle.

(MARSHALL *snorts.*)

But I'm the only one round here who hasn't anything to hide.

KAY. Are you, now. Then you're very lucky. You're a very lucky man, Fitzpatrick. If you don't mind me saying so.

FITZPATRICK. No. I don't mind. I probably am. You're right.

(MARSHALL *laughs.*)

KAY (*unruffled*). And you think that, then, has some virtue.

FITZPATRICK. Aye. I think it probably has. Meaning no disrespect whatsoever, (*indicating* BENNETT) it was Bennett who pointed out the fact with which, until then, we were unacquainted. Namely that you, Kay, yourself, had been in clink. So what ... ?

MARSHALL. Some of my best friends are criminals.

FITZPATRICK. What I can't abide is a man who can point his finger at other people but can't bear the same one to be pointed at himself.

KAY. Some people, Fitzpatrick, have injuries that go deeper than you imagine.

MARSHALL. Oh, very nice. (*Applauds discreetly.*) He got that from a book.

FITZPATRICK. I mean, glass houses, Kay. Glass houses. There's not one now you can't see here. Just by turning round.

(MARSHALL *turns round.*)

KAY. That's very fine, Fitzpatrick.

MARSHALL. It is. I agree with that myself.

KAY. Do you put a price on anything, Fitzpatrick?

FITZPATRICK. I don't know. I put a price on the work I do here. Minimal it may be, but I do put a price on that.

MARSHALL. Come on now, then. Let's get back to work. (*Rubs his hands.*)

FITZPATRICK. And one other thing. A little more civility might have been more becoming.

MARSHALL. It would.

FITZPATRICK. We're not just here, now, to be pushed around.

KAY. It looks to me, Fitzpatrick, that you've come here – this morning like any other – to cause trouble wherever you can ...

FITZPATRICK (*looking at* BENNETT). If a man puts his fist in my face I'll be damned if he doesn't get one back. Wherever that man might come from.

BENNETT. And you think that's something to admire, Fitzpatrick?

FITZPATRICK. No. No. It's not admiration at all I'm after. (MARSHALL *laughs.*)

KAY. I think you better get home, Fitzpatrick.

FITZPATRICK. What?

KAY. I think you better get off. Come into the office at the end of the week and you'll get whatever you're owed. (*Silence. Then:*)

FITZPATRICK. Huh. (*Looks round for his jacket.*) Do you mean that?

KAY. I do.

(FITZPATRICK *goes to his jacket. He slowly pulls it on.*)

FITZPATRICK (*to* MARSHALL). Are you coming?

MARSHALL. Well, now ... If there's one of us to be out of work ... better that the other sticks to what he can.

FITZPATRICK (*bitterly*). Aye. I suppose you're right.

(*He goes to the door.*)

It's amazing, you know ... the way he surrounds himself with cripples. (*Gestures at the house.*)

KAY. Cripples?

FITZPATRICK. Yourself ... Bennett ... Glenny ... Marshall ...

MARSHALL. Fitzpatrick ...

FITZPATRICK. And lastly of course, myself. It qualifies, I suppose, the nature ... of his warm and understanding heart. Ah, well. You can tell him one thing for nothing. The road up yonder is a harder climb than that. (*Thumbs upwards*.) I'll say goodbye. May God go with you, and treat you more kindly than Himself. (*Taps* GLEN- DENNING *on the shoulder as he goes*.) Watch it, Glenny. One day, mind ... (*Gestures hammer with his hand*.)

GLENDENNING. Aye! (*Laughs*.)

(*As he goes to the door* EWBANK *comes in*.)

EWBANK. And where the hell do you think you're going to? God Christ. Just look at the time. Knocking off and they've only been here half an hour.

FITZPATRICK. I've been fired.

EWBANK. Don't be so bloody silly. Get on with this bloody walling ... God damn and blast. Just look. Covered in bloody muck. *Marshall* ... *!* (*Gestures at* MARSHALL *to get on with the floor*.) Fitzpatrick ... let's have it up. (*Indicates floor*.)

(*Slowly they go back to their tasks.* KAY *alone doesn't look up*.)

Kay, let's have these battens out ... Good God. We're going to be here all night.

KAY. Bennett ...

MARSHALL. The couple got off to a happy start, then, Mr Ewbank.

EWBANK. What? ...

MARSHALL. The happy ...

EWBANK. Mind your own bloody business. Bennett, I don't call that working. (*To* MARSHALL) How the hell would you know that?

MARSHALL. I ... Me ... We ...

FITZPATRICK. Ah, but a great day. Celebratin' ...

EWBANK. I'll celebrate my boot up your bloody backside, Fitzpatrick. That's what I'll do ... God Christ. God Christ. They come in here and start telling you what sort of night you've had ...

KAY. Bennett, over here ...

(*They work, silent, taking out the battens and the last of the floor.* EWBANK *grunts, groans, murmurs to himself.*
They watch him, glancing at one another, as they work.
Then:)

MARSHALL. Married life. There's nothing like it. You can't beat it. Though I do say so myself.

EWBANK. Lift it. Lift it. Lift it. God Christ, they think you live here, you know, like they do at home ...

MARSHALL. They do. They do. That's right. A bloody pigsty. He knows.

EWBANK. Flat on their backs all night. And flat on their bellies all day long to go with it ...

MARSHALL. He was sacked, nevertheless, Mr Ewbank. Demoted.

EWBANK. There's been nobody sacked from this firm since the day it first began. God Christ, Kay, I've heard some bloody tales in my time, but that one takes the can.

FITZPATRICK. Ah, it's a great life if you can afford it.

MARSHALL. And what, now, is that?

FITZPATRICK. A wife. Home ... children.

GLENDENNING. I ... I ... I ... I ... I ... I ... I ...

MARSHALL. Hot chocolate by the fire.

FITZPATRICK. Hot chocolate by the fire.

GLENDENNING. I ... I ... I ... I ... I ... I ...

(EWBANK *mumbles and groans to himself, unnoticing, then:*)

EWBANK. If you took my advice, Kay, you'd bloody well get shut ...

KAY. What ...

EWBANK. Four lasses. Good God. You ought to have more common sense ... A man your age: you ought to have more bloody common sense ... God Christ.

GLENDENNING. I ... I ... I ... I ...

EWBANK. That's all right, then ...

(*The men take out the battens.* KAY *is working, loosening them.*)

God. Bloody orchestra. Kay, you should have seen it. Dressed up like a cockatoo. There'll be some of them stretched out still, out yonder. I shouldn't be surprised. God Christ. You've seen nowt like it.

FITZPATRICK. Had a damn fine time, did you, an' all?

EWBANK. Who's asking you?

FITZPATRICK. I thought ...

MARSHALL. Married life. You can't beat it.

EWBANK (*to* KAY). Made me speech standing on the bridegroom's table ... Just look at that. (*Gestures at the ground.*)

MARSHALL. On the other hand, Mr Kay here has been telling us how he's been to prison. Enjoyed the experience, he said, no end ... Regaling us you know with all the sordid details.

EWBANK. Tipped half a bottle over some chap's head ... Bloody waiters. Chef ... If you can't for one day in your life enjoy it.

FITZPATRICK. And not left a drop of the damn good stuff for us.

EWBANK. What's that?

FITZPATRICK. I say, Kay here isn't one to make a fuss.

EWBANK. By God, bloody embezzlement. That'd make 'em shift, Kay. Four lasses.

MARSHALL. Embezzlement?

EWBANK. By God. There's nowt for him to embezzle here.

(*Laughs.*) Ay bloody hell. You need a firework up your arse. Just look at that ... Get on. Get on. Here, I'll give you a lift myself.

FITZPATRICK. Embezzlement. Now there's a wonder.

MARSHALL. And all the time now...

FITZPATRICK. One of us.

MARSHALL. Hiding his light beneath a bushel.

FITZPATRICK. Along, that is, with the cash from someone else's tub.

(MARSHALL *and* FITZPATRICK *laugh.*)

EWBANK. What's that?

MARSHALL. I say, your son's not out to help us, then, this morning.

EWBANK. No. He's not.

FITZPATRICK. Ah. It's a great life if you can mix it.

EWBANK. He's off on his bloody travels.

MARSHALL. Travels?

FITZPATRICK. Abroad, is that?

EWBANK. I wouldn't know if you told me ... He's never in one place two minutes running.

FITZPATRICK. Ah, travelling. A great broadener of the mind.

EWBANK. A great emptier of the pocket, if you ask me, more likely.

(OLD EWBANK *has come in at the back.*)

FITZPATRICK. Don't worry. One day he'll settle down.

EWBANK. Will he? That's your opinion, Fitzpatrick?

FITZPATRICK. Modern times, Mr Ewbank. The up and coming generation.

EWBANK. Aye, well. They can up and come all right ... You can start loading that bloody lorry, Kay. Let's have 'em out.

FITZPATRICK. The world of the imagination ...

EWBANK. Is that what it is, Fitzpatrick?

FITZPATRICK. The ferment of ideas.

EWBANK. If he'd ferment something out of it we shouldn't be so bad.

MARSHALL. Like a damn good liquor ...

FITZPATRICK. Like a damn good Scotch. You're right.

> (*They go, taking the last of the battens with them.* BENNETT *remains, starting to strip the ropes on the centre poles.*
>
> *After a while, as* OLD EWBANK *talks,* MARSHALL *and* GLENDENNING *return to wrap the walling, laying it out on the ground at the back of the tent and folding it, seam on seam.*)

OLD EWBANK (*to* BENNETT). Did I show you that rope the other day?

BENNETT. What? I don't ...

OLD EWBANK. In the house. I keep it there.

BENNETT. Aye. I think I saw it ...

OLD EWBANK. Four hundred feet some days. By hand.

BENNETT. Aye ...

OLD EWBANK. What? You saw nothing like it.

BENNETT. Aye. That's quite a lot.

OLD EWBANK. Horses? Damn it all. Sheep-nets ... Fishing boats ... Dogger Bank. Iceland. Scapa Flow ... *Greenland*. You'll find bits of rope I made you know, floating under the North Pole. Good God. A piece of rope in those days ...

BENNETT (*still working*). Aye ...

OLD EWBANK. Balloons? Do you know once they used it on an airship. Bigger than a house. Damn it all. You could go anywhere with a bit of rope. (*Suddenly confidential*) I know. Don't you let these people mislead you.

BENNETT. Ah, well. I better get on with this.

OLD EWBANK. They haven't the strength to stand up. A bit of an ache and they're dashing for a pill and a sup from a bottle. They haven't the appetite you know, for work ... There's one sat out there now, on the back of the lorry, eating a damn great cake. I've never seen so many people sitting down, eating ... Have I showed you my rope?

BENNETT. Aye.

OLD EWBANK. Twelve? Eighteen. Sometimes twenty hours a day. Good God, you'd no time to sit eating. When I married my wife I never used to see her but one day in four.

MARSHALL. Those were the days, Benny, right enough!

OLD EWBANK (*turning to* MARSHALL). Steam? By God, there was!

> (EWBANK *has returned, followed by* KAY.
> FITZPATRICK *has already come back and is laying out the walling.*)

EWBANK. Come on, now. Let's have it folded.

OLD EWBANK. I can't stop now. I'm just going for my walk.

> (OLD MRS EWBANK *has come in.*)

Got used to it, you know. Used to walk twenty or thirty miles a day. It'd take ten miles walking to make a hundred foot of rope.

OLD MRS E. I've been looking for you all over. Do you realize you haven't got on any socks? (*To* EWBANK) Has he been here long?

EWBANK. He's just arrived. He'll be all right.

OLD MRS E. (*reprovingly*). He's been out walking. He'll catch his death of cold.

MARSHALL. He's a fine old man, missis.

OLD MRS E. He needs looking after. That's a fact.

OLD EWBANK (*to* BENNETT). One day in four. Five if I worked over.

OLD MRS E. (*looking round*). It's amazing how soon they disappear ... (*To* EWBANK) We're off in half an hour.

EWBANK. I'll come and see you ...

OLD MRS E. Aye ... Well, I'll take him in. Get him dressed. (*Shouts in* OLD EWBANK's *ear.*) I'll take you in!

OLD EWBANK. What? We've only just started.

OLD MRS E (*going, her arm in* OLD EWBANK'*s*). He still thinks we're having the party.

OLD EWBANK. God damn and blast. When you tied a knot it'd take you a fortnight to unravel it.

(*They go.*)

EWBANK. Get packing this walling up ... Let's have it out.

(*They start to pack the walling. The others are removing the last side poles.*)

FITZPATRICK. The lucky couple are on their travels, then?

EWBANK. Aye. Aye, that's right ... Shan't see them again for a damn long time.

FITZPATRICK. A doctor ...

EWBANK. Aye.

FITZPATRICK. The medical profession. It's a fine thing, to have a vocation in life.

EWBANK. And what's one of them when you've got it at home?

FITZPATRICK. Why, I'd say Kay, here, was a vocated man.

MARSHALL. That's right.

FITZPATRICK. An air of dedication.

EWBANK. Dedication ... He knows which side his bread's buttered on. Isn't that right, Kay? So's all the rest of them, an' all.

FITZPATRICK. Aye. We're all pragmatists at heart.

EWBANK. Pragmatists, is it? Bone bloody idle. There's nobody else round here'd employ any one of you as far as I can make out.

MARSHALL. Ah, now. That's a fact ...

FITZPATRICK. The debris of society ... That's us.

EWBANK. Watch that bloody lacing ...

(MARSHALL *and* GLENDENNING *are lacing the bag of walling;* BENNETT *goes to relieve* GLENDENNING.)

BENNETT. Here, let me have it ...

(*He and* MARSHALL *carry it out.* FITZPATRICK *follows them, taking side poles;* GLENDENNING, *after glancing round, goes out after them.*

PAUL *has come in as the last of the work is being done; now he comes down the tent, casual. He wears a coat.*)

PAUL. Well, then, I'm off.

EWBANK. By God, then ... Look at this.

PAUL. All up ... all finished.

KAY. Just about.

EWBANK. Crawled out of his bloody hole ... (*To* KAY, *who's now taking off the quarter guys*) Seen him last night ... wouldn't believe it ... Comes up here, you know, for the bloody booze ... nowt else ...

PAUL. That's it. Just about.

EWBANK. By God. Nomads, Kay, that's us ... Tenting ... First tent I ever had, you know, caught fire ... went up ... should have seen it ... Went up ... (*Pauses, abstracted.*) Off, then, are you?

PAUL. That's right.

EWBANK. Aye ... (*Gazes at him.*) Back up, I suppose, when you need some money.

PAUL. Manage by meself.

EWBANK. Aye ... Still to see it.

PAUL. Alus a first time.

EWBANK. Aye ... can just imagine.

PAUL. Well, then ...

(*Pause, gazing over at one another.*

FITZPATRICK *comes in, followed by the others.* GLEN-DENNING *carries a little sack with which he goes round, picking up litter from the grass.*)

FITZPATRICK. So you're leaving us behind.

PAUL. Aye. That's right.

FITZPATRICK. A wandering spirit. I know the feeling well ...

PAUL (*laughs*). I can imagine.

FITZPATRICK. Aye. I'm a born traveller. Circumstances alone conspire against it.

MARSHALL. On the Dublin to Liverpool express.
(*They laugh.*)

FITZPATRICK (*to* BENNETT). Being a single man, I know the temptations very well.

MARSHALL. You don't know where you're off to, then?

PAUL. Oh ... (*Shrugs.*)

FITZPATRICK. I'll give you one piece of sound advice.
(PAUL *looks up.*)
For nothing now. If you're ever tempted, at any time, to marry ...

MARSHALL. Don't.

FITZPATRICK. Not until you're far too old.

MARSHALL. Not until you're far too old.

PAUL. I'll try and remember that ... Goodbye, Glenny.

GLENDENNING. I ... I ... I ... Aye! (*Nods his head.*)

PAUL. See you some time.

GLENDENNING. Aye!

PAUL. Well, then ... (*Looks over at* EWBANK.)

EWBANK. Aye. I'll walk with you to the house ... (*To* KAY) When you let it down keep it clean. No bits and pieces ...

KAY. Right ...
(EWBANK *goes with* PAUL, *who waves to the others and they call out as he goes.*)

FITZPATRICK. They had a great time then, last night.

MARSHALL. Aye. You can tell it by his manner.
(*They laugh.*)

FITZPATRICK. It's a great feeling. (*Stretches.*)

MARSHALL. What's that?

FITZPATRICK. To feel reinstated.
(MARSHALL *laughs.*)

KAY. You can get the rest of this out now ... (*Indicating remaining flooring*) And start loading the truck.

FITZPATRICK. Aye, aye, sir! (*To* MARSHALL) See that?

MARSHALL. It's a great man who knows his place.

FITZPATRICK. You're right, Marshy. It is that.

(*They take out the last side poles, and any remaining pieces.*

KAY *and* BENNETT *work alone, untying the laced edges of the canvas, prior to taking it down. The edges of the canvas are supported now only by the four corner side poles.*

BENNETT, *aware suddenly that he and* KAY *are alone, wanders over to the view of the valley.*)

BENNETT. It's amazing, isn't it. The number of chimneys they can put into a place the size of that.

KAY (*unlacing canvas*). Aye.

BENNETT. They'll soon be gone.

KAY. What's that?

BENNETT. Central heating. They don't need chimneys, you know, for that.

KAY. Aye.

BENNETT. Just roofs you'll see.

KAY. And aerials.

BENNETT. Aerials?

KAY. Television.

BENNETT. Oh, aye ... You can just see a car. Going up the other side. Sun shining on its window ... Look ... Gone.

KAY. I shouldn't let Fitzpatrick worry you.

BENNETT. No.

KAY. Gets under your skin. (*Watching him*)

BENNETT. Aye ... Well, I suppose you have to laugh.

KAY. Aye. (*Nods.*)

BENNETT. The thing is ... I suppose one day, I'll bloody kill him.

KAY. Aye.

(*They laugh.*

The others start coming back.)

KAY (*as* FITZPATRICK *and* MARSHALL *come in*). Right, then.
Let's have it down.

(*They go to the poles,* FITZPATRICK *rubbing his hands,*
spitting on them.)

FITZPATRICK. Nice to know, now, that we're speaking.

MARSHALL. Ah, Kay's not the one to hold a grudge ... A spot
in jail would do us all the world of good.

FITZPATRICK (*fingering canvas*). Damn fine stuff ...

(*They take the ropes.*)

FITZPATRICK. Easy come. Easy go.

MARSHALL (*lowering rope*). Benny, now: his old man.

(FITZPATRICK *and* MARSHALL *laugh.*)

ALL. Ready!

KAY. Right, then ... Let's have it down.

(*They've taken the ropes holding the canvas, and take the*
ends outside the tent, at each of the 'quarters'. At KAY's
signal they release the hitches holding the ropes at the foot of
the poles and the canvas slowly descends. As it comes down
they rip the lacing, working towards the centre poles,
separating the three pieces of canvas.

Then, as the men unshackle the canvas:)

GLENDENNING. I ... I ... I ... If I had a ... had a ... had a ...
had a son ...

FITZPATRICK. Aye? Aye? What's that?

GLENDENNING. If I ... I ... I ... I ... had a lad I w ... w ... w
... wouldn't have him w ... w ... w ... wandering off.

BENNETT. What's that, Glenny?

GLENDENNING. I ... I ... I ... I ... I ...

MARSHALL (*sings*). Ay, yi, yi, yi ... Ay, yi, yi, yi ...

GLENDENNING. I'd have him a ... a ... a ... at home.

H

FITZPATRICK. At home, would you?

GLENDENNING. W ... w ... w ... w ... working.

FITZPATRICK. Aye, well, lad. That day might come.

MARSHALL. Son and daughter, Glenny.

GLENDENNING. Aye!

FITZPATRICK. Though there's one thing, Glenny.

GLENDENNING. Aye!

FITZPATRICK. You'll have to stop 'em eating.

MARSHALL. Meal-times, now, and nothing else.

GLENDENNING. Aye!

>   (*The men have unshackled the canvas and now begin to fold it.*)

MARSHALL. A big fat cream bun, now ...

FITZPATRICK. Once every Christmas.

GLENDENNING. Aye!

MARSHALL. And the odd kiss at bedtime, Glenny, for the wife. (*Winking*)

GLENDENNING. Aye! (*Laughs, pleased.*)

FITZPATRICK. He'd make somebody a good husband would Glenny.

GLENDENNING. Aye!

MARSHALL. Either that, now, or a damn fine wife.

>   (*They laugh.*)

FITZPATRICK. I read in the paper once about this place where all the women live together ...

MARSHALL. I can just imagine that. I can ...

FITZPATRICK. And all the men in another place entirely ...

MARSHALL. And they pass over there ...

FITZPATRICK. That's right ...

MARSHALL. At night.

>   (*They laugh, wrapping the canvas.*)

FITZPATRICK. Had families like you have chickens ...

MARSHALL. Broilers ...

FITZPATRICK. Or those cows that never see the light.

MARSHALL. And all the man had to do was his day's work. The rest of the time was all his own.

KAY. Suit one or two people I could mention.

BENNETT. Suit one or two people here. You're right.

(KAY *and* BENNETT *laugh.*)

MARSHALL. Bennett, on the other hand, of course, is a different case entirely.

FITZPATRICK. 'Tirely.

BENNETT (*to* FITZPATRICK). Aye ... They'd create a special post for you.

KAY. One to lean up against, I'm thinking.

BENNETT. Aye. One to lean up against ... you're right.

(KAY *and* BENNETT *laugh.*)

FITZPATRICK. Hey ...

MARSHALL. Hey, now ...

FITZPATRICK. There's a provocation.

KAY. That's right ... (*To* BENNETT) Without a bloody doubt.

(KAY *and* BENNETT *laugh.*

Behind them EWBANK *has come back with a bottle and several glasses on a tray, together with several small pieces of wedding cake.*)

EWBANK. Here, now. You've not finished. Get it off, now, and we'll have a drop of this ... Glenny. Fetch us in a table.

GLENDENNING. Aye! (*He goes off.*)

(FITZPATRICK *and* MARSHALL *exchange looks; the men have begun to bag the canvas and lace it in the bags.*)

KAY. What about the poles, now? (*Looking up*)

EWBANK. Leave them now for the other truck. They'll never fit on this one ... Now go damn careful with that. (*Indicating canvas*) By God, that was bloody quick.

(GLENDENNING *has gone out and come back in with a white metalwork table.*)

EWBANK. Mention food and you can't see him for dust.

MARSHALL. He's smelled that cake.

FITZPATRICK. He has.

EWBANK. Now off, lad. Let's see you working. It won't run away, don't worry. (*He puts the tray on the table.*) It'll still be here when you've finished.

BENNETT. It's a lovely view you have here, Mr Ewbank.

EWBANK. Aye. And it costs a tidy drop, an' all.

BENNETT. I never thought of that ... (*Looking towards the house*)

EWBANK. There's no compensation, I can tell you, for being saddled with a lot of brass.

MARSHALL. Aye. Those of us without it have a great job remembering.

EWBANK. You're a damn sight better off without ... Ask Kay. He'll tell you. (*They laugh.*)

FITZPATRICK. Aye. Aye. We could ask him that.

BENNETT. Your lad's gone then, Mr Ewbank, on his travels?

EWBANK. Aye ... He has. His mother's wept bloody buckets. I don't know why. He'll be back again tomorrow.

FITZPATRICK. It's a great thing to have. The spirit of adventure.

EWBANK. There's only one spirit that I know of and you don't have to travel far for that.

(*They laugh.* EWBANK *remains impassive.*)

KAY. Come on, Fitzpatrick. Let's have a bit of carrying ...

EWBANK. Aye. Let's tidy up the lawn.

(*They carry the canvas out.*

GLENDENNING *returns with his bag and wanders round the lawn, picking up the pieces of paper streamers.*)

KAY. Well, then. I think that should do it.

EWBANK. Aye ... (*Looks round.*) Left a few damn marks.

KAY. I suppose it has to be reckoned.

EWBANK. Aye ... You pay a price for everything, Kay. Best
not to look, then you never know whether you've got it,
or you've gone without ... (*Calling off*) Put it straight, for
for Christ's sake. All that lot'll bloody well fall off. (*To*
KAY) There's one thing, though ...

KAY. Aye?

EWBANK. Ah, well ... (*Uncertain for a moment. Then:*) I came
out here, you know, this morning ... Saw it all ... Damn
near broke my bloody heart ... You saw it. God. What a
bloody mess ... Seen nowt like it. I haven't.

KAY. S'all made to be used.

EWBANK. Aye. You're right. Doesn't bear much reckoning.
Best get on with it while you can.

KAY. Aye. (*Laughs.*)

EWBANK. Did you see much of my son?

KAY. No ... Not much.

EWBANK. What do you reckon to it, then? Do you know,
I've lived all this time—and I know nowt about anything.
Least ways, I've settled that. I've come to that conclusion.
(*He laughs. Shakes his head.*) A bloody wanderer.

KAY (*watches him. Then:*) Your lad?

EWBANK. I've no idea at all. None. Do you know? ... Where
he's off to. I don't think he has himself. His mother sits at
home ... (*Shakes his head.*) The modern world, Kay. It's
left you and me behind.

KAY. Aye. Well. It can't be helped.

(*They are silent a moment. Then:*)

EWBANK. Pathetic. (*He looks round.*) A lot of bloody misfits.
You could put us all into a string bag, you know, and
chuck us all away, and none'd be the wiser.

KAY (*laughs*). Aye. I think you're right.

EWBANK. Aye. (*Laughs.*) Sunk without trace.

(MARSHALL *comes in, rubbing his hands.*)

MARSHALL. Ay, now. That's just the stuff you want ... (*To*
GLENDENNING) Tickle your bloody tonsils.

GLENDENNING. Aye!

(*Follows* MARSHALL *over to the table.* BENNETT *also
comes in.*)

EWBANK. Never changes. Tell 'em there's summat here
needs shifting and you'll be bloody hollering all day long.
Show 'em half a bottle and they'll knock you over where
you stand.

KAY. Aye! (*He nods and laughs.*)

MARSHALL. Had a drop of this before we started and we'd
have been over in half the time.

EWBANK. Aye. I know. Over the lawn, more likely. Stretched
out, flat on your back. (*He's pouring a liberal portion into
each glass.*)

FITZPATRICK (*coming in*). A lot of holes you have in here ...
(*Looking round*)

EWBANK. Aye. Well. It'll grow again. Come today. Gone
tomorrow.

BENNETT. Everything in its season.

EWBANK. Aye. That's right ...

BENNETT. This time next year ...

MARSHALL. Bloody philosopher.

BENNETT. I had a lawn of my own once ... (*Pauses.*)

EWBANK. Here you are, then. Hand it round ...

(*They pass round the glasses and* EWBANK *holds out the
plate with the cake.*)

FITZPATRICK. Nay, Glenny, lad ... This isn't for you.

MARSHALL. Make your ears drop off.

FITZPATRICK. Your tongue drop out.

MARSHALL. Black hairs sprout up all over.

GLENDENNING. Aye! (*Takes his glass.*)

(*They laugh.*)

KAY. Here's to your good health, then.

MARSHALL. And the happy couple.

BENNETT. Aye, and the happy couple.

FITZPATRICK. And to ought else now that you have in mind.
(*They laugh. Drink.*)

MARSHALL. By God. But that's a mighty drop of stuff.

FITZPATRICK. That'll curl your bloody whiskers.

BENNETT. Aye!

FITZPATRICK. Still all there, Glenny, are they?
(*They laugh.*)

GLENDENNING. Aye!

MARSHALL. You better count them. We don't want you
leaving, now, without.

GLENDENNING. Aye!

FITZPATRICK. He's a damn fine lad. (*Arm round* GLENDEN-
NING's *shoulder*)

MARSHALL. He is. He is. You're right.

BENNETT. And that's a lovely drop of cake, too, to go with it.

KAY. It is. It's very good.

GLENDENNING. I ... I ... I ... I ... I ...

FITZPATRICK. He's after another.
(*They laugh.*)

EWBANK. Nay, lad. That'll have to do you.

KAY (*putting down his glass*). Right, then. We better be getting
off.

EWBANK. Aye. I'll be down to the yard later ... Make sure
you've packed that load right, Kay.

KAY. Aye ... (*He goes.*)

EWBANK. Drive carefully. Drop nowt off.

FITZPATRICK (*setting down his glass with* BENNETT). Ah,
that was a damn fine drop. I won't say that I couldn't
stand another ... But then, work's work.

EWBANK. Aye. And don't you forget it.
(FITZPATRICK *goes.*)

MARSHALL. See you at the yard ... (*Sets down his glass.*)

EWBANK. Aye. Aye. That's right.

BENNETT. Thanks again, Mr Ewbank ...

EWBANK. ... nothing of it.

> (BENNETT *goes with a nod.*)

Go on, Glenny. Get off, or they'll leave you here behind.

GLENDENNING. Aye!

EWBANK. Sithee. I've a bit extra for you. (*Takes a bit of cake from his pocket.*) E't it now when they're not looking, or they'll have it off you.

GLENDENNING. Aye!

EWBANK. Right, then. Off you go.

> (GLENDENNING *goes, eating.*
> EWBANK *is left alone.*)

FITZPATRICK (*off*). Come on. Come on, now. My turn in the cab.

KAY (*off*). On the back, Fitzpatrick.

FITZPATRICK (*off*). Good God.

MARSHALL (*off*). He'll be blown away.

BENNETT (*off*). Some hopes of that.

MARSHALL (*off*). Ay, now. There's no room for me up there.

KAY (*off*). Are you right, then, Glenny ... ?

GLENDENNING (*off*). Aye!

FITZPATRICK (*off*). Here he is. He's here.

MARSHALL (*off: sings*). Ay, yi, yi, yi ... Ay, yi, yi, yi ...

> (*Laughter. Dies away.*
> *Silence.*
> EWBANK *stands alone, gazing out from between the poles. Fastens ropes hanging from the pulleys, almost absent-mindedly, abstracted. He gazes at view again.*
> *After a while,* MRS EWBANK *comes on. Silent a moment, looking round.*)

MRS EWBANK. They've gone, then.

EWBANK (*doesn't look up*). Aye.

MRS EWBANK (*pause*). You get used to the noise around you after a while.

EWBANK. Aye. You do.

(MRS EWBANK *gazes across at the view.*)

MRS EWBANK. Your mother and dad are leaving in a few minutes.

EWBANK. I'll come and see them off.

MRS EWBANK. He's lost his bit of rope.

EWBANK. I'll cut him off a bit. He'll never know the difference.

MRS EWBANK. ... All that smoke ... Like a carpet ... They had a drink, then.

EWBANK. Aye. Wet the baby's head ... (*Looks up at her expression.*) Well, I don't know, do I? These days ... one damn thing ...

(*Pause. Then:*)

Set an example there'll be no stopping. They'll be wanting a sup on every job from now on ... I don't know. (*Looks down at the view, standing beside her.*) You'd think you'd have something to show for it, wouldn't you. After all this time.

MRS EWBANK. Well, now ... (*Abstracted*)

EWBANK. I don't know ... (*Looks round. Then down at the lawn*) Made a few marks in that.

MRS EWBANK. One or two ...

EWBANK (*shivers. Looks up*). Autumn ...

MRS EWBANK (*abstracted*). Still ... It's been a good summer.

EWBANK. Aye. Comes and goes.

MRS EWBANK. What ... ?

(*Pause.*)

EWBANK. Do you know that Kay was had up once for embezzlement?

MRS EWBANK. They've been had up for a lot of things. The men that work for you.

EWBANK. Aye ... Nobody else'll have 'em ... I must be bloody daft. Well. I suppose we better see the old uns off.

MRS EWBANK. Yes ...

EWBANK. I don't know ... What's to become of us, you reckon?

(MRS EWBANK *looks at him, smiles, then shakes her head.*)
Never do this again, you know.

MRS EWBANK. No ... (*She smiles.*)

EWBANK. Me heart wouldn't stand it.

MRS EWBANK. No ... (*She laughs.*)

OLD MRS E. (*off*). Frank ... !

EWBANK. Aye, well. (*Half-laughs.*) That's summat.

(*They turn slowly, arm in arm.*)

OLD MRS E. (*off*). Frank ... !

EWBANK. S'all right. We're coming. (*To* MRS EWBANK)
Well, then. We better go.

(*They go.*
The stage stands empty: bare poles, the ropes fastened off.
The light fades slowly.)

CURTAIN